PRAISE FOR
UAPs and the Nuclear Puzzle

"*UAPs and the Nuclear Puzzle* will help inform the public and move us forward on our journey towards a new understanding of history, UAP, and of our own true nature with respect to the larger reality that is revealing itself to us."

—LESLIE KEAN, bestselling author, *UFOs: Generals, Pilots, and Government Officials Go on the Record*

"I can't overstate the significance of military testimony from witnesses such as former launch control officer Robert Salas. It's brave folks like him that have kept me pushing for further government transparency on what may turn out to be the biggest story in modern times."

—JAMES FOX, director/producer, *Moment of Contact*

"Salas takes the reader on a compelling and heartfelt journey through the minefields and thickets of government secrecy and cover-ups as he experienced it from his own encounters with ETs, while weaving into his page-turning narrative a concise history of the modern UFO phenomenon."

—THOMAS J. CAREY, bestselling coauthor of *UFO Secrets Inside Wright-Patterson*

"A sober yet heartfelt narrative which dares you to dismiss it without due consideration."

—*FORTEAN TIMES*

"Fasten your seat belt. You are in for a fascinating ride."

—STANTON T. FRIEDMAN, author, *Flying Saucers and Science* and *Captured! The Betty and Barney Hill UFO Experience*

"Not only is Bob Salas an Air Force insider who had his ufological teeth cut by firsthand experiences, but he also possesses the scholarly background to analyze those events. With his tireless tenacity and no-nonsense mission towards disclosure, Bob is a genuine throwback to one of my own heroes, Edward Ruppelt."

—DONALD R. SCHMITT, bestselling coauthor, *Witness to Roswell*

UAPs *and the*
Nuclear Puzzle

Visitations,
National Security,
and the Need for Transparency

ROBERT SALAS

FOREWORDS BY **STANTON T. FRIEDMAN** AND **LESLIE KEAN**

NEW
PAGE

This edition first published in 2023 by New Page Books, an imprint of
Red Wheel/Weiser, LLC
With offices at:
65 Parker Street, Suite 7
Newburyport, MA 01950
www.redwheelweiser.com

ISBN: 978-1-63748-016-8
Library of Congress Cataloging-in-Publication Data available upon
request.

Cover design by Sky Peck Design
Cover photograph © iStock.com/MicroStockHub
Interior by Happenstance Type-O-Rama
Typeset in New Baskerville, Andrade Pro, and Bell Gothic

Image on page 26 is an official USAF photo.
Images on pages 27 and 123 are USAF images, provided under the
    FOIA.
Images on pages 30 and 49 are courtesy of the author.
Image on page 36 copyright *Great Falls Tribune.* Used by permission.
Image on page 124 courtesy of John Mullican.
Image on page 125 courtesy of Rex Heflin.
Image on page 126 © 2014 Larry Lowe. All rights reserved. Used by
    permission.
Image on page 134 obtained via FOIA request.

Printed in the United States of America
IBI
10 9 8 7 6 5 4 3 2 1

My journey into the subject of UFOs that resulted in this book could not have been possible without the encouragement and loving companionship of my wife, Marilyn. There have been many times that I have wanted to extricate myself from further involvement in this complex subject because I thought I had done and had enough. Marilyn has consistently encouraged and motivated me to continue to pursue the cause of disclosure of my story and the reality of this phenomenon. I am very grateful for that encouragement because it has given me a sense of greater understanding and acceptance of the phenomenon. I dedicate this book to her; to the conscientious investigators; and to the millions of people who have found themselves witnesses to the UFO phenomenon and who are still searching for answers.

CONTENTS

FOREWORD

I read my first book about UFOs, *The Report on Unidentified Flying Objects,* way back in 1958, primarily because it was by an Air Force officer, Edward J. Ruppelt, who had been the head of the USAF Project Blue Book in the early 1950s. I had needed to order one more book from the mail-order house to get free shipping, and it was a hardcover book marked down from $2.95 to only $1.00. It basically was free. I was a young nuclear physicist working for General Electric on the Aircraft Nuclear Propulsion program and certainly at that time respected the USAF, which, with the Atomic Energy Commission, cosponsored the program. As I have wended my long weary way to being a full-time ufologist, fifty-six years later, I have read a great many other UFO books. Frankly, many of them weren't much good, even if often they were sent to me for review. So it was, in contrast, a great pleasure to read Robert Salas's *book.* I just wish he had written a longer one, because I found his approach fresh and sensible and based on serious study and an impressive background.

I have complained for many years that both believers and nonbelievers in alien visitations really don't know much about national security and how the government works. Robert Salas indeed knows about security. He also has a solid background as a graduate of the US Air Force Academy. Add to that his work at a high-tech, very highly classified location—a Minuteman Missile launch facility. Personnel at such facilities undergo psychological testing to assure that the staff near the missile launch button are sane. And he has spent much of the past twenty years researching flying saucers. He had a very intriguing UFO experience relating to the "impossibly" rapid shutdown of ten Minuteman Missiles armed with nuclear warheads. There was a UFO over the front gate. Put it all together and we have a fascinating book.

He had also demonstrated a great deal of courage in being willing to come forth to talk about the experience at Malmstrom AFB and also what seems to have been a strange but fascinating abduction experience. He has an excellent section on the US government intelligence world, which works so hard to keep secrets from the public about UFOs and many other topics. Hard to imagine, but there are sixteen different US government intelligence agencies.

I share Robert's concerns about all the nuclear weapons sitting in the nine countries that have joined the nuclear club. Obviously, he is aware of the terrible destruction that would ensue if somebody started a nuclear war. He is also clearly aware of how little prepared the world is for such a catastrophe. He talks about some UFO cases with which I was not familiar. I was, as a nuclear guy, also intrigued by his comments about science fiction writer H. G. Wells, who used the term "atomic bomb" way back in 1914 in his book *The World Set Free*. The neutron wasn't even discovered until 1932, and the first nuclear chain reaction not demonstrated until December 1942. And I always associated Wells primarily with the 1938 radio broadcast of *The War of the Worlds* starring Orson Welles. Farsighted he certainly was. So fasten your seat belt. You are in for a fascinating ride.

STANTON T. FRIEDMAN

FOREWORD TO
NEW EDITION

I'm honored that Robert Salas invited me to follow the late Stanton Friedman in contributing a second foreword to this new edition of his book, now titled *UAPs and the Nuclear Puzzle*. Stanton has already described Robert's outstanding credentials and background. Most importantly, Robert was directly involved with one of the most significant and well-documented national security UFO events ever, which formed the foundation of his long investigation and personal journey. Despite his grounding in the military and his scholarly coverage of history, Robert takes all genuine UFO witnesses and experiencers seriously. He brings an unusual openness and respect to this aspect of the phenomenon that is so often cast aside. All these elements are interwoven within his longstanding effort to bring about change.

The UFO/missile incident at Malmstrom Air Force base in 1967 occurred before the issuance of the Air Force "fact sheet" at the close of Project Blue Book, which we now know—thanks partly to Robert's coming forward—was far from factual. Rather, it was issued to perpetuate a cover-up. Robert has dedicated decades of his life to undoing the knot of that cover-up.

As a journalist covering UFOs, I have been fortunate to have known Robert Salas for over twenty years. His contributions through writing, speaking, and research, and those of his colleagues who were involved with similar incidents, have been of immeasurable importance. Robert's 2005 book *Faded Giant,* coauthored by James Klotz, brought his years of investigation into the public arena and provided a wealth of government documents obtained through the Freedom of Information Act. This work was of great benefit to me when writing my 2010 book *UFOs: Generals, Pilots, and Government Officials Go on the Record,* which included an interview with Robert about the Malmstrom event and its implications.

However, my admiration for Robert goes beyond his investigation of this incident. He has also been deeply committed to the larger effort calling for government transparency and disclosure. He is acutely aware that excessive secrecy threatens the survival of our democracy, keeping the public in the dark about one of the most important issues facing all of us. This has threatened public trust in government, and is continuing to do so.

To address this problem, Robert recently founded the Unidentified Aerial Phenomenon Action Committee (UAPAC) to help provide oversight of congressional actions going forward. "Congress enacted laws to require more openness about UAP," the group's 2022 press release states. "However, it remains to be seen how the Pentagon and the intelligence community will respond to the ground-breaking legislative requirements." I couldn't agree more, and I commend Robert for setting up a group to potentially provide assistance to whistleblowers who may face unforeseen difficulties when they come forward under the new legislation.

UAPs and the Nuclear Puzzle goes beyond a study of unidentified aerial phenomena (UAP) by providing a rich historical context. This background—which is interesting unto itself—helps us understand the mechanics and perils of our reliance on nuclear weapons. Robert makes it clear that the stockpiling of these weapons as a deterrent is not only a risk to our survival but also has implications for any off-world civilizations in our neighborhood. He describes shocking case summaries of encounters with the anomalous objects at nuclear bases during the cold war and afterwards.

In addition, Robert does not shy away from taking his narrative into the stranger world of alien encounters, sharing what he believes to be the purpose and intentions of the nonhuman beings visiting our planet. He discusses cases that go from the highest level of the military all the way to reports of farm boys conversing with visitors from landed spaceships. The combination of his meticulously researched factual reporting with an acceptance of the presence of nonhuman visitors, woven into the text in a pragmatic and straightforward style, struck me as something unique. The "weird" is not treated as such; it simply is part of the whole.

But that's not all. Robert is courageous enough to take his readers even farther. He recalls an encounter with a being in his bedroom, and acknowledges that he, too, is an experiencer, like so many others. This personal exposure reflects not only his integrity, but also is of extreme importance in offering support to the many experiencers from all walks of life who have suffered in silence or have been ridiculed for speaking out. Perhaps this book will help change the cultural perspective on these mysterious, disturbing events that need to become a part of the larger conversation.

To some, UAP are not just a national security threat, as portrayed by the military in the narrative so prevalent now. They can be perceived as a threat on a personal level, often with medical or psychological effects. And, when these powerful, highly advanced technological objects impact the larger structure of global societies, the threat becomes existential as it challenges the stability of our anthropomorphic sovereignty. Or, perhaps they are no threat to us at all. Robert offers a possible, and hopeful, outcome to disclosure that could unify us as a planetary civilization.

I was one of the authors of the December 2017 *New York Times* story about a secret Department of Defense UFO program, which initiated a new level of official engagement with UAP. Since then, official acknowledgment that UFOs are real, physical, unexplained objects that do not appear to originate in the United States or any foreign country has marked the beginning of a new era. A government task force has been designated to look into UAP and provide reports to the public; Congress held its first public UAP hearing in over fifty years; and legislation is likely to pass mandating further protection for potential whistleblowers.

Still, we have a long way to go. Secrecy prevails. *UAPs and the Nuclear Puzzle* will help inform the public and move us forward on our journey toward a new understanding of history, UAP, and of our own true nature with respect to the larger reality that is revealing itself to us.

LESLIE KEAN

NOVEMBER 2022

PREFACE

I feel obligated to write this book, partly because it is about an injustice. Like many of you, I have had my share of living with injustice. Like many of you, I have observed too much intolerance, greed, self-gratification, disrespect, violence, and hatred. You are my brothers and sisters; this is my planet; this is my country and my government; this is my life and I am going to try to do what I can to reveal the truth and help bring about more understanding and mutual respect, so that we can continue to evolve together to a higher plane of existence. Only then will we be ready to fully accept the reality of a universe that is teeming with precious life, as is our planet.

There are two things I know with certainty about the UFO phenomenon. One is that the phenomenon is real. That is, real objects of unearthly origin are visiting our airspace and our planet. My second certainty is that the phenomenon of people being abducted by sentient beings, who are operating these unknown craft, is also a reality. These conclusions do not come from hypotheses, guesses, theories, or concepts that I have used to convince myself of these realities. They come from my life experiences. They are facts that many of you reading this have not yet accepted in your own minds. I have had the benefit of that conscious knowledge gained from my experiences. I must admit, however, that these resolute conclusions did not happen overnight. Although I was well aware of the facts of my own UFO incident, it was a multiyear, multidecade process to come to terms with these realities. For most of my life, I have thought of myself as a thoughtful and rational individual. I have achieved some academic success. I have an innate love of mathematics and an appreciation for the logical thinking process that mathematics helps us to develop. I did not arrive at these conclusions lightly or quickly. Ultimately, confronted with the entire body of knowledge from my own experiences and the experiences of others, I could come to no other conclusions.

Having accepted these realities, other possible realities present themselves. Not the least of these is that secret groups must exist within world governments, including our own, that are also well aware of these truths. And because there has been no official public declaration by any of them of the UFO reality, they are all effectively in collusion with each other in hiding these facts from the general populace.

Sometimes, it is easy to perceive our government as some living entity that has some good and evil tendencies, with multiple personalities and objectives. The US "government," as it stands today, has evolved over a period of almost 250 years. It has evolved from the conflicts of political personalities, wars, strikes, financial collapses, disasters, and its laws. In short, it has come to be what it is as a result of the totality of the events during its time. It is definitely not my intent to paint our government as possessing some evil, conspiratorial intent against its citizens. We simply need to recognize that it is a work in progress, as it has been since its beginning.

I worked for the US. government for nearly thirty-two years. I can assure you that the vast majority of federal employees are honest, hardworking, and dedicated to doing the best they can in service for our country. The government is not the issue. We, the people, are the issue. Can we people really hold our government accountable for its secrets? Can we change its behavior if we deem it necessary? Can we work together to confront the reality of UFO phenomena? These and other questions are still to be answered. However, before we can make real progress with the daunting task of government accountability regarding the UFO phenomenon, we must educate ourselves with the information that is available to us. As part of that education, I simply offer here a review of my own experiences and thoughts about this complex, fascinating phenomenon. I also gratefully include some pertinent comments by many other researchers and witnesses.

The phenomenon is not a simple mystery that can be solved once you have some key evidence. It is not a separate and distinct puzzle. This involves a complex series of puzzles that we have had to confront since we looked up at the night sky and wondered. We are both cause and effect for this mystery. What we perceive as something that has evolved from our sightings of unidentified flying objects, something from "out there," is really about us and our relationship with the "out there." Ultimately, we have no choice but to find the answers we need in order to deal with it. I invite you to continue reading this book to completion because I have put into it what I know about the phenomenon—beyond a reasonable doubt.

INTRODUCTION

What model in the natural world could we use for the assembly of nations that we now have on this planet? Maybe we could use a flock of geese as a model. There is usually a lead goose that the others follow in formation. Somehow that seems too orderly and too simplistic for our complicated world of nations. If that were a good model, we would have true leadership and peaceful cooperation among the members. We would all know where we are going.

Maybe a better model would be something like a galaxy of stars. Stars are formed out of the chaotic motion of nebular gas and particles that are the remains of stars that finished their life cycle in an explosion. Stars within a galaxy are in motion around a central core that contains a black hole. They are kept in the galaxy by the gravitational attraction of other stars. There is a wide variety of sizes and luminosity among stars. Sometimes stars collide with and absorb each other. Out of the seeming chaos of the cosmos, there is some order. There is that word "order" again, and therein lies the difficulty in using the galaxy as a model.

The nations of the Earth, during all recorded history, have never been able to coalesce into an orderly state of being. There may be no good natural model for the world of nations as it is today. It may be that the world of nations will always be in a constant state of volatile change. You and I and billions of other people are the caretakers—the movers and the modelers of this world of nations. Do we have a plan? Are we headed in the right direction? Will we have answers in the near future? I think we all need to take time to contemplate these questions, because we all must be part of the answers.

The United States has pulled all of its soldiers out of Afghanistan, but there is still a hope that we will somehow help that country evolve into a democratic state and an ally. In addition, there was the "Arab Spring" in the 2010s, and waves of uprisings against totalitarian governments are still occurring among the peoples of numerous Middle Eastern countries. And, although there has been an attempt to limit the growth of nuclear-weapons states, there remains the real possibility that Iran and others will soon be in a position to develop their own nuclear arsenal. The nations of the world don't know where they are headed, and there seems to be no end to the chaotic conditions of the world.

Having uncertainty in world affairs is nothing new. Human history is full of situations of impending doom. What is new, however, is the criticality of conditions and situations in which we humans find ourselves today. If these are not addressed soon, they could seriously threaten our civilization as we know it. Two examples of extremes we face are the continuing crises over nuclear weapons and runaway global warming. There are others that also require our immediate and *coordinated* attention and action. Unfortunately, *coordinated action* is still a concept we are trying to learn. One major detractor that severely hinders our working cooperatively is extreme secrecy in governments.

My objectives for this book are to review the secrecy— the distortion of the truth by governments—about the extraterrestrial life that is visiting our planet, and us. It is mostly about us—our perceptions and our fears and how we are learning to accommodate this knowledge. It is also about being true to our ideals as we struggle to define what it means to be human.

One of the first important books on the subject of UFOs provides us insight into the early phase of this phenomenon. *The Report on Unidentified Flying Objects* by Air Force Captain Edward Ruppelt was published in 1956. Ruppelt was the first director of Project Blue Book from 1951 to 1953. This was the last publicly identified Air Force project involved with the UFO subject. Blue Book ended in 1969. By the time he was in charge of Blue Book, it had already undergone a major shift by the Air Force, from making a sincere effort to understand the phenomenon to the cover-up and a disinformation posture.

Ruppelt had read the history from the earlier versions of Blue Book, Project Sign (1947–1949) and Project Grudge (1949–1951). He notes that by the end of 1947, the consensus of those investigating UFOs for the Air Force was that they were interplanetary. Even Dr. Vannevar Bush, the chief government scientific advisor, stated that the idea that UFOs were produced by earthly science was impossible. In fact, the highest levels of our government did know for certain that these were interplanetary, because they had already recovered extraterrestrial craft and beings from the 1947 Roswell crash in New Mexico.

Evidence of the beginnings of an extensive cover-up by a secret group is also presented in Ruppelt's book. He writes that in September 1948, the Air Force Project Sign investigators wrote a TOP SECRET "Estimate of the Situation" report on the UFO question. This report concluded that UFOs were interplanetary. When this was presented directly to the Air Force chief of staff, Hoyt Vandenberg, it was rejected as not based on any real proof. Because Vandenberg, as Air Force chief of staff, would certainly have known about the Roswell recovery, clearly he and the intelligence community had decided to maintain two realities about the subject. They needed the more public Air Force project to keep reviewing UFO activity while the "secret group" would continue doing the real, in-depth analysis under the protection of the highest levels of secrecy.

By mid-1949, according to Ruppelt, there was a major change in attitude at ATIC (Air Force Technical Intelligence Center—Wright-Patterson Air Force Base). He makes this telling observation: "This change in the operating policy of the UFO project was so pronounced that I, like so many other people, wondered if there was a hidden reason for the change. . . . This period of 'mind changing' bothered me. Here were people deciding that there was nothing to this UFO business right at a time when the reports seemed to be getting better. . . . Maybe I was just playing the front man to a big cover-up" (Ruppelt 1956, 36–37).

The objective from 1949 was to put an end to UFO reports. "Project Grudge had a two-phase program of UFO annihilation. The first phase consisted of explaining every UFO report. The second phase was to tell the public how the Air Force had solved all the sightings" (Ruppelt 1956, 38). However, this attempt to put an end to public interest in the subject failed completely. After the major flap regarding sightings over the Washington, DC, area in 1952, Ruppelt met with a group of Air Defense Command officers. He quotes them as saying: "None of us can understand why Intelligence is so hesitant to accept the fact that something we just don't know about is flying around in our skies—unless you are trying to cover up something big" (Ruppelt 1956, 256).

What was becoming clear to those in Project Blue Book was that the official and the unofficial Air Force policies on UFOs were decidedly different. The Air Force had obviously made some decisions on how they would handle this subject, then and in the future. There would be a dualistic approach. There would be a very serious and very secret effort to learn as much as possible about the phenomenon and set a course of action for dealing with it. In addition, there would be a more open, official, token effort to look into the phenomenon for the sake of public consumption and for those in government who did not have a need to know. Our intelligence organizations were well versed in this method of protecting secrets. They had just succeeded in protecting the secret of the atomic bomb during its development. And that was accomplished while thousands of people worked on the project collaboratively. The blueprint for operating a secret group was already in existence.

There were other significant outcomes of the 1952 Washington, DC, UFO flap. One was that the order was given to pilots intercepting UFOs to "shoot them down"

(Feschino 2007, 46). There was no official announcement to the public that the occupants of UFOs were being declared enemies of the United States, but the order to shoot at these unknowns entering our airspace had been given, and once given, permission to fire on these objects would be the (unofficial) policy.

Another result of the 1952 flap would be the hardening of the government's approach to the problem of extraterrestrial craft flying in our airspace. Our intelligence agencies would now take the lead in setting the course of action regarding these strange objects. That was made clear when in January 1953 the CIA organized a secret meeting of selected scientists whose only agenda was to discuss the UFO problem. This was the Robertson Committee Panel. Much of what was discussed in that meeting remains classified. However, information that has been released indicates that part of their solution for handling the UFO problem would be to establish a disinformation campaign to discredit the phenomenon. This has proven to be an effective strategy in keeping the UFO question in the realm of incredulity in the mind of the public.

CHAPTER 1

A Nation of Secrets

"Secrecy is a form of government regulation . . . it is generally the case that government prescribes what the citizen may know."

—*REPORT OF THE COMMISSION ON PROTECTING AND REDUCING GOVERNMENT SECRECY* (MARCH 1997)

In December 1960, I was a freshman cadet at the US Air Force Academy in Colorado. By then, I knew how to follow orders without asking questions, and I knew that keeping military secrets was highly important. One evening in early December, the entire corps of cadets was ordered to attend a classified briefing. During that briefing, we were told that there were US military advisors on the ground in Vietnam helping the South Vietnamese army fight against the invading Communist North Vietnamese army under Ho Chi Minh. We were also shown film footage of that effort.

It was emphasized during our briefing that we were only there in an advisory capacity and not actually participating in the fighting. I don't think any of us believed that, even then. This briefing was only days before John F. Kennedy assumed the office of the presidency. Therefore, the mission of the "advisors" had to have been planned under the Eisenhower administration. Kennedy had not initiated our involvement there, as many might assume from the unclassified accounts of the Vietnam War during that era; he inherited that war from those who preceded him.

Why was the corps of cadets informed of our involvement in Vietnam at that time? My guess is that our commanders were preparing us for our potential involvement in that war. That bit of motivation had to have come from the top of the military chain of command. The writing was already on the wall. We would have another war.

Of course, the fact that we were involved implied we were on the right side of that foreign conflict. What we were not briefed on was that, years earlier, the CIA had made the decision to manufacture that war and choose the sides (Trento 2001, 327–342). After the defeat of the French army at Dien Bien Phu in 1954, an armistice was signed in Geneva. It was agreed that Vietnam would be divided at the 17th parallel. North Vietnam was to be controlled by the government of Ho Chi Minh, which had allied itself with Communist China, and the South would be in the hands of the dictatorial Bao Dai. This Geneva Accord provided for "free" elections for all of Vietnam by 1956. This plan was an attempt by the UN to avoid another war. However, within the offices of the US policymakers, such as Ike's secretary of state and former CIA director Allen Dulles, plans were being made to insure the right outcome of that election. Part of that plan was to bring Ngo Dinh Diem, a Catholic Vietnamese expatriate who had been living the high life in France, back into the country. And, to insure his election, the CIA was given a blank check to bring as many Catholic Vietnamese from the North as it could muster. In addition, there would be a generous bribe for Bao Dai to step down.

The election of Diem was only part of the plan. After his election, a strong military organization would have to be developed to provide a defense against the eventual attempt at a Communist takeover by the North. It was obvious to the CIA then that there would be a war over South Vietnam. The CIA would plan and initiate the preparations for it in secrecy. Under the guise of "military assistance," the CIA organized the Military Assistance Advisory Group (MAAG) to help the South Vietnamese army prepare for war. The CIA plan for a democratic regime in South Vietnam collapsed when Diem began persecuting the Buddhist majority. The end result of these secret CIA operations would be the senseless and bloody Vietnam War. Thirty years later, history would essentially be repeated in the run-up to the Bush-era Iraq War.

In 1965, I volunteered for duty in Vietnam. They could not assign me right away, so in the interim, I was offered the assignment for missile duty. I accepted that assignment and, as I was about to leave for training, my request for a combat assignment in Vietnam was approved. I was offered a choice of either assignment, because at that time both assignments were critical needs of the Air Force. As I was considering these options, some fellow officers had returned from Vietnam and strongly encouraged me not to get involved in what they saw as an unnecessary and mismanaged war. They had some convincing arguments, so I chose missile duty.

There are lessons to be learned from this brief recollection about the beginnings of the Vietnam War. In the world of government secrets, there are secrets within secrets. Secrets can easily become complex, and the original intent can become corrupt. Much of the information previously described would not be known if it were not for the unauthorized public disclosure of the Pentagon Papers. Major US policy decisions, especially war plans, are initiated under the cloak of secrecy before they are open for public discussion.

There is no question that government secrets are necessary for the protection of our country and its citizens. The human population has managed to separate itself into a world of distinct countries, flags, national anthems, goals, and many other distinguishing features. That nationalism has resulted in the need to protect and defend our borders and those distinct features by which we identify ourselves. We humans have created a competitive mentality against all other countries. As a result, we keep secrets not only to protect ourselves from an attack, but also to give ourselves some perceived advantage. We have certainly seen that with our insatiable quest for superior armaments. It is an easy argument to make that if a potential enemy—literally any other country in the world—has access to information about our strengths or weaknesses, then we have put ourselves at a disadvantage and are vulnerable to attack. Such was the case at Pearl Harbor before the start of World War II. This argument certainly validates the basis for national security secrecy.

When I was granted access to secret information while serving in the Air Force, I remember the dual sense of importance and dread I felt. I was being given a secret that could be "vital to the interests of the national security of the United States of America." Those kinds of words are powerful and strike a sense of pride in anyone who loves his country. And, if you are a young man or woman proud to wear the uniform and proud of being a defender of your country, those words inspire a strong allegiance and dedication to keeping the secrets. The dread I felt was the thought of breaking that bond, letting my country down, or disgracing myself as a traitor to my country and going to prison. Any of those outcomes would certainly have resulted in an abject feeling of lost personal self-esteem. Those are stark, deeply emotional motivators that instill a personal commitment to keep the secrets.

Clearly, World War II was the kind of war where democratic nations were at extreme risk of being defeated and their peoples subjected to tyrannical rule. Military power and influence were at their zenith during that period, and rightly so. When that war ended in 1945, the possibility of a war with Communist nations was of great concern. The fear that had gripped us during World War II would define the postwar period. It resulted in further solidifying the structure and influence of US intelligence agencies. By 1947, secrecy in government operations had become entrenched. One of our prized military secrets of the war, the blueprint for the atomic bomb, was now in the hands of our new enemy, the USSR. The Central Intelligence Agency would be established and espionage would become the front line of defense in a new war, called the Cold War. It would be a war of secrets.

It was during this period that the Roswell incident occurred. The world intelligence community certainly had knowledge of strange flying craft. They were well aware of the so-called "foo fighters" appearing in the skies during the war. Though they knew of the existence of these strange craft, it is likely that US government did not yet have an actual craft to study, and therefore had some questions as to the origin of these craft. It was in that environment that a craft of extraterrestrial origin crashed near Corona, New Mexico, in 1947.

Many books have been written about the Roswell incident. One of the better-researched accounts is *Witness to Roswell* by Thomas Carey and Donald Schmitt (2009). I won't review the incident; however, there are some aspects of the accounts that are relevant to this discussion. Within days of the crash at the Foster Ranch near Corona, and before Major Jesse Marcel, a US Army Air Force intelligence officer from Roswell Army Air Field, arrived at the debris field, many ranchers and residents in the area knew about the crashed disk. After Marcel reported the very unusual finding to his superiors, it was apparently concluded by Colonel William Blanchard, commander of the 509th Bomb Group, that the debris and the crashed disk, located some twenty-eight miles from the debris field, was indeed a flying saucer craft of unknown origin. He proceeded to direct his public information officer, Lieutenant Walter Haut, to issue a press release stating these very findings. It was not until the next day that this announcement was rescinded by his commander, General Roger Ramey. That quick reversal of "facts" established the birth of the UFO cover-up that we are still experiencing today.

It is important to note that Colonel Blanchard understood that such a momentous discovery—of a craft and living creatures not from Earth—should be announced to the world immediately! The fact that his superior officer rescinded his announcement does not detract from the fact that he tried to do the right thing. Whether or not this ET craft was part of an alien invasion, the public had a right to know about it. However, the powers in Washington disagreed. In their view, the public did not have the right or need to know this truth! Also of note is that Blanchard later became a four-star general and deputy chief of staff of the Air Force.

Notwithstanding the denial, the Air Force still had a major problem on its hands. Literally hundreds of people had either seen the debris, the saucer, or pieces of it, or had heard someone they trusted speak about it. Some of these people were military personnel and could be easily muzzled. However, many were civilians. What could be done to keep the civilians quiet?

In fact, the military was well versed on how to keep the civilian population from disclosing military secrets. World War II had established the American military's superiority in the eyes of the world and in the eyes of all Americans. In addition, Roswell Army Airfield was the home of the 509th Bomb Wing, the bomber group that had dropped the atomic bomb on Japan to end the war. This base, its officers, and its men evoked a real sense of pride in the people of Roswell. The decision was made not just to *ask* those people to keep quiet about the saucer crash but to *demand* their silence.

According to witnesses, many of whose testimonies are documented in *Witness to Roswell*, they were threatened with their lives, and the lives of their children and even their grandchildren if they spoke openly about what they knew. These threats came from officers and men in uniform, representing the government of the United States! There have been so many of these reports that I have to conclude these allegations are probably true. As a result, we are also led to conclude that elements within our government have had the will to use extreme measures to cover up this secret. It is worth reviewing this again so as not to minimize its import.

By December 1946, the United States knew Soviet spies had infiltrated the nuclear laboratory at Los Alamos as early as December 1944. Our greatest military secret, the atomic bomb, had been compromised by our most recognized enemy, Stalin's USSR. On July 26, 1947, the National Security Act was signed, which restructured the military establishment and created the National Security Council and the CIA. Clearly, the country was in a high state of postwar anxiety over its security. The Roswell incident occurred in the first week of July 1947, at a time in our history when there seemed to be a crisis surrounding national security and the resulting secrecy in government. It seems that whenever such a perception of crisis occurs within the halls of government, extremes of thought and actions take hold. For example, even though nuclear war should be an unthinkable option in any rational discussion, the use of nuclear weapons has been given serious consideration at various times in our history. (Some of these will be detailed in a later chapter.)

Many other examples prove the point that extreme measures birthed and carried forth by government are not unusual. In this case, these extreme actions involved the intentional threats of death by our government agents against our own citizens. And for the reason of keeping secret the fact that extraterrestrial visitation had indeed occurred. We would see extremes in interrogations and control of witnesses again in other UFO cases such as the RAF Bentwaters (UK) incident in 1980.

There is no rational justification for what has been perpetrated against witnesses to UFO phenomena. Some of these extreme measures were purely and simply illegal behavior by our government.

Referring to nuclear energy, David Lilienthal, the first chairman of the Atomic Energy Commission, once warned about the effects of overzealous security on the American people: "There is a growing tendency in some quarters to act as if atomic energy were none of the people's business. In my opinion, this is plain nonsense and dangerous nonsense. . . . If schemers or fools or rascals or hysterical stuffed shirts get this thing out of the people's hands, it may then be too late to find out what it is all about" (*Secrecy 1997*).

This comment would certainly apply to the UFO phenomenon. It is the kind of government thinking that says: "This is too important to allow the people to know about it." So stifling are the effects of the secrecy extremes our government has taken in the name of national security interests that conscientious individuals in government are unwilling to take the responsibility for conclusions that they themselves could draw from available and unclassified sources. However, if the people who are privy to these irresponsible actions continue to allow it, then they, too, are complicit.

PSYCH JOB

In June 1969, I was transferred from Malmstrom Air Force Base in Montana to Wright-Patterson Air Force Base in Ohio. I was told that this transfer would allow me to complete my master's degree at the Air Force Institute of Technology. I wanted to stay at Malmstrom because the facilities and staff for completing the master's program were still available at the base. It made little sense to me why I should be ordered to complete this program at Wright-Patterson, but the orders were cut for my transfer and I went. It was not long after I arrived at Wright-Patterson that I happened to encounter an officer whom I had first met at the Air Force Academy. He had been an upperclassman, and I hadn't seen him since he had graduated in 1963. As an upperclassman, he, along with his roommate, had made a special effort to make my life there as difficult as he could during my first year. They had honed their hazing techniques to a science. However, when he approached me at Wright-Patterson, he was very friendly and welcoming. He said he was happy to see me!

Now, this guy had treated me miserably when we were at the Academy, and I had not seen him since then, so I was shocked by his friendliness at this meeting. We spoke briefly but as he left he said to me that he wanted to speak with me later about a possible assignment after graduation from the Air Force Institute of Technology. I asked him about the type of job he had in mind. He simply said we would speak later about it.

It was not too long after that meeting that I received a telephone message ordering me to report to the base psychiatrist's office at the base hospital. I thought this was a strange order because I had not complained of any psychological problems to anyone. When I tried to speak with the psychiatrist's office about this, the orderly simply confirmed that I was expected to report for a meeting with the base psychiatrist. I reported on the appointed day. As I was sitting in the waiting room, I again told the orderly that I had no reason to be there. He said it was out of his hands. When he came to me and told me that the doctor would see me, I simply told him I would not go back to see the doctor unless he came out and explained to me why I was there. The orderly, being outranked, said he would ask the doctor about this. He came back after about fifteen minutes and simply told me that the appointment was no longer required and that I could leave. I have always felt a sense of relief that I did not see that psychiatrist.

Much later, after I went public with my story and became more involved with researching the phenomenon, I wondered about the meaning of these incidents. I have now come to believe that there could have been a couple of outcomes if I had gone back to see the psychiatrist.

The first outcome could have been that a discussion about my UFO experience at Malmstrom (see chapter 2) would have come up and it would have been put in my medical record as a way to keep me quiet about the experience. If I had then talked about this case while in the Air Force, it would have compromised my military career. A second outcome could have been that they, including the officer who had been with me at the Air Force Academy, may have been trying to recruit me into working for the Air Force intelligence side of the UFO phenomenon. The Condon Committee had just finished its final report in February 1969, and the Air Force was about to announce they would no longer investigate UFO reports. That announcement would allow the Air Force to continue their investigations of phenomena in secrecy, without public scrutiny. I think I made the right decision not to see that psychiatrist.

My next assignment after Wright-Patterson was at the Space and Missile System Organization (SAMSO) at the Los Angeles Air Force Station. There I worked as a reliability engineer on the Titan III missile propulsion system for the Titan III systems program office. I worked on this program for little more than a year. Some months before I decided to resign from the Air Force in 1971, I was asked to meet with my immediate commander. He told me that there were inquiries about me from the Air Force group handling the highly classified projects for SAMSO.

These were the people we called "spooks." What I understood about their work was that they developed spy satellite requirements and specifications for other space-based programs. I was invited to meet with them for a possible position in their organization. However, I decided I'd had enough of dealing in highly classified material so I declined the offer to meet with them. Again, I simply speculate about the possibility that I was again singled out, due to my Malmstrom incident, to be a part of the Air Force cover-up in an effort to keep me quiet.

It was soon after that when I decided to resign my commission from the Air Force. I made this decision primarily because I was against the continuation of the Vietnam War.

At that time, I thought I had put my incident behind me as a vague memory of something I could not explain to myself. My next employment was in the aerospace industry, where I briefly worked for Martin-Marietta and then Rockwell International as a reliability and safety engineer. In 1973 I went to work for the Federal Aviation Administration in aircraft certification, specializing in aircraft structures. I worked in that field for more than twenty years. In 1995, I finally retired from government service. Before resigning from FAA, I began a master's in education program at the University of Washington.

In 1994, while browsing through the UW bookstore, I came upon a book that would dramatically change my life: *Above Top Secret*. On page 301 was a brief paragraph that read, in part, "In the spring of 1966 the command and control consoles of a launch control center in Great Falls, Mont., indicated that a fault existed in each of the ten missiles simultaneously. . . . An identical incident occurred during the week of 20 March 1967" (Good 1988, 301).

ADDENDUM—OCTOBER 2022

As a result of reading this brief paragraph and my belief that the incident of the week of March 20, 1967, was the one I had experienced, I decided to take a chance that the Air Force had declassified it and released documents under the Freedom of Information Act (FOIA). I contacted an investigator from the Mutual UFO Network (MUFON), James Klotz, in April 1994 and asked him to submit a request for information on the Echo shutdown but not to mention anything about UFOs. As a result of this effort, the Air Force did declassify the "Echo Flight" incident, which involved a flight of ten missiles becoming disabled due to "undetermined reasons."

Though the memories of my incident were vague, I had no knowledge of any other similar incident during the time I was at Malmstrom, so I believed, after reading the documentation we received, that this *was* the incident I had experienced. I felt a great sense of liberation from the secrets I had been holding about my direct experience with this phenomenon. I began a multiyear process of recovering memories and obtaining facts that led to the realization there had been two such incidents within the span of eight days!

The paragraph in *Above Top Secret* mentioned two incidents at Malmstrom AFB: one in 1966 and one during the week of March 20, 1967. From my research, I was unable to confirm any such incident occurring in 1966 at Malmstrom. However, it should be noted that there was a similar incident involving the shutdown of ten missiles at Minot AFB in September 1966. When we received the FOIA documents, the date of the Echo incident was March 16, 1967, a Thursday. This was certainly not the week of March 20, which was the following Monday. When I received the notes of Dr. Roy Craig (see photo below), the investigator for the Condon investigation, the date of March 24 was quoted many times, mistakenly referring to the Echo incident.

However, as would later be confirmed to me by the personal testimony of Robert Jamison, the officer in charge of restarting the Oscar Flight missiles, along with testimony from my own commander, Fred Meiwald, it was actually the Oscar Flight that was disabled on March 24, 1967.

This handwritten note by Craig confirms that a flight of missiles was disabled on March 24 as related to him by Ray Fowler. The reasons the Oscar Flight incident is not mentioned in the documentation we received under FOIA are likely due to the higher level of secrecy that was instituted by the Air Force after the Echo Flight incident occurred. I did not specifically request documents on the Oscar incident initially because I was unaware that there were two separate incidents. As will be discussed later, the Condon Investigation was in progress at the time of these incidents, and the Air Force did not want to alert them or provide any details for these highly significant incidents.

CHAPTER 2

Faded Giant—Revisited

In October 1966, the US secretary of defense announced that the Air Force had selected Dr. Edward U. Condon and the University of Colorado for the UFO research contract. Also in October 1966, Lieutenant Frederick Meiwald and I became certified as a missile combat crew. We received a Highly Qualified rating during our qualification check. Of course, at that time we had no idea there would be a nexus between our crew and the Condon Committee Investigation.

We served together for about a year, until I became qualified as a missile crew commander. During that year, we kept our Highly Qualified rating. I spent the remainder of my three years at Malmstrom as a crew commander. Fred Meiwald continued his career in the Air Force and at one point held the position of deputy base commander at Offutt Air Force Base in Nebraska, the headquarters of the Strategic Air Command.

We pulled "Alert" duty about once every three days. The routine was that we would attend a morning briefing where we would be informed about any scheduled maintenance activities and any reports of a technical nature, such as modifications. It was generally uneventful.

Sometimes, in the winter, especially when the weather turned bad, we would all have to drive to the Launch Control Facility (LCF) through deep or blowing snow. Montana winters can be brutal. At times, we would be flown by helicopter out to the sites.

After arriving at the site, we would check in with the main security guard, called the flight security controller (FSC). Security is, of course, paramount at these sites because we had operational control of nuclear weapons. We were issued sidearms at that point, and we continued to an elevator that took us to the lower level of the site where the Launch Control Center (LCC) or "capsule" was located. We followed strict authentication procedures before the crew on duty would open the huge blast door and allow us entry. Once inside we would follow additional procedures to complete the crew changeover. Once we inspected the capsule and settled in, it was generally a quiet afternoon and evening of monitoring the weapons systems and any ongoing maintenance or security activities.

It was on one of those quiet evenings when the event occurred that would eventually precipitate my deep interest in the UFO phenomenon and become a part of my life for many years to come. Most of the details of that event of March 24, 1967, are in my book *Faded Giant* (Salas and Klotz 2005). I will briefly review the details of the incident at Oscar Flight.

Sometime that evening, I first received a call from my flight security controller (FSC). He said simply that he wanted to report some unusual "lights" that were flying above the facility. He said that he and other security personnel had been observing them for a short while. He went on to say that the lights were unusual in that they were making maneuvers that aircraft could not do. They would move at high speed, stop abruptly, then reverse course and hover, and they were making no sound. In listening to this report, I certainly thought it strange and even said, "You mean like UFOs?" I should note that there had been recent reports of strange lights in the sky in news articles printed in the *Great Falls Tribune*. To that, he said that he couldn't explain the lights and simply wanted to report them to me. I thanked him for the report and said to let me know if anything more significant occurred.

After ending that call, I admit thinking that it was unusual to receive this kind of report. Our communications with "topside" (our security crew at ground level) were usually very professional. Obviously, our security people were very familiar with the night sky over Montana. However, I did not give it much thought. Then, within minutes of that call, I received another call. This time the FSC was screaming into the phone, clearly fearful and agitated. He said there was one of those lights hovering just above our front gate. He kept talking in a highly agitated voice and said he had all the guards at the ready with their weapons drawn and wanted me to give him instructions on what to do next. I'm not sure what I told him because I was still startled by the call, but I do remember telling him to ensure that nothing entered the perimeter of the facility. He quickly hung up the phone after saying that one of his guards was injured. Later, the FSC told me that the guard had been injured due to a cut on his hand that he suffered from attempting to climb the perimeter fence.

At that point, I realized something serious was going on topside. There was some sort of attempt in progress to enter our facility. And, of course, our facility had the responsibility to secure the nuclear weapons under its control. I immediately turned to wake Meiwald, who was sleeping on the cot behind me. Before waking him, I recall briefly pausing to look at my display of lighted indicators on our missile status board, just to check their status. Although I knew something serious was going on topside, I had the distinct feeling that something was about to happen to the missile systems. As I was about to tell Meiwald about the calls, we began to get audible alarms and indicator lights on our status board. All of our missiles were indicating NO-GO; they were all disabled.

Colonel Fred Meiwald

This was astonishing to us because there was no way to create this condition external to our control center in the underground capsule. Our equipment had somehow been tampered with from outside the capsule!

The Oscar Flight launch control facility. Photo courtesy of James Klotz.

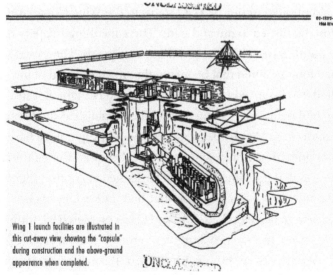

Wing 1 launch facilities are illustrated in this cut-away view, showing the "capsule" during construction and the above-ground appearance when completed.

Cutaway of Wing 1 Launch Control Center

Although I will refer the reader to *Faded Giant* for additional details, there is one more important aspect to recount.

First, I will note that when I initially tried to recall the incident of that night, I struggled to remember some details. It had been nearly thirty years and there were a lot of other memories in between. In addition, I had made a conscious effort to forget the incident when I was ordered (in writing) not to discuss any of it with anyone, ever. I had tried to follow those orders, even into civilian life. Another point here is that each of the LCCs looked identical. For these reasons, and the fact that I later became a crew commander whose home LCC was November Flight, I was initially unsure of where the incident had occurred.

In *Faded Giant* (page 13), I state that my incident at Oscar Flight occurred on March 16, 1967, the same day as the Echo Flight incident. The reason I had thought that was the case is because I had a very specific memory. After Fred Meiwald phoned in our NO-GO status to the Wing Command Post, he turned to me and said, "The same thing happened at another flight!" I recalled those very words. Therefore, I had long assumed that he meant that the same kind of incident had occurred (at Echo Flight) that very night. Because we had definitive documentation that established the Echo shutdown as March 16, I reasoned that our flight must have also gone down on that date. In fact, what Fred meant to say was that the same thing had happened at another flight about a week earlier, as was what had, indeed, happened. Echo went down on March 16 and Oscar on March 24, while UFOs were in close proximity to our missile launch facilities.

At the time James Klotz and I finished writing *Faded Giant* in 2004, there were still some outstanding questions. One question was the exact date of the Oscar Flight shutdown. We had received no documentation from our Freedom of Information Act (FOIA) requests relative to the Oscar shutdown. By the time I discovered that I had been in the Oscar capsule at the time of my incident, I had already gone public, and the Air Force realized that this was a UFO-related incident. The document flow from the Air Force dried up. We also did not know why Oscar Flight was not mentioned in any of the reports of the Echo Flight investigation. More importantly, I did not understand the significance of these incidents in relation to the ongoing Condon Investigation, and how deep and flagrant was the Air Force cover-up. The testimony of one witness became the key to helping with these two important questions.

In 2010, Robert Jamison appeared alongside six other witnesses at the National Press Club in Washington and presented his testimony about events related to the Oscar Flight shutdowns. Lieutenant Jamison was a targeting officer assigned to the 341st Missile Maintenance Squadron. His principal job was to ensure that missiles were properly restarted and brought back to alert status after undergoing maintenance. In his affidavit, he states that he was called out one evening to restart the Oscar Flight. It was verified to him that all ten missiles at Oscar Flight had gone NO-GO and that it had been reported by the security guards at the facility that a UFO had been seen just prior to the malfunction of the missiles. According to a 2010 affidavit, Jamison's team was ordered to "remain at the hangar, as a precaution, until all UFO reports from the field had ceased."

Robert Jamison at the National Press Club

He estimated that he'd had to wait two to three hours before being given the go-ahead to proceed to Oscar Flight. While waiting, he recalls being told about the UFO seen that evening over Belt, Montana. This was a close sighting by a truck driver and a Montana Highway Patrol officer and is well documented in a Blue Book file. (This case will be reviewed in more detail later.) The date of that sighting was March 24, 1967, which thereby establishes the date of the Oscar Flight shutdown.

In his affidavit, Jamison goes on to say that he and all the targeting teams received a "special UFO briefing" prior to each dispatch for the next two weeks. They were instructed to report any UFO sightings to the Missile Command Post and to undertake self-defense measures in the event that a UFO made a nearby appearance while they were performing missile repairs in the field. He was also told about the Echo Flight shutdowns due to UFO encounters about a week earlier. It should be noted that

Bob Jamison spoke to researcher Robert Hastings about this information in 1992, two years before I went public about the Oscar Flight shutdowns.

These statements certainly contradict the statement in the Wing Unit History for the period: "rumors of Unidentified Flying Objects (UFO) around the area of Echo Flight . . . were disproven" (Gamble 1967, 38).

I don't know how these "rumors" were disproven. The rumors were certainly not disproven by Airman Smith (pseudonym). Smith was a targeting technician who was a member of the team assigned to bring Echo Flight missiles back to alert status. After a search of missile maintenance personnel who might have been in the field during the UFO incidents, Smith was located in 2004 by researcher James Klotz. Smith agreed to discuss his experience because he considers public disclosure of the details as highly important to the understanding of this phenomenon. However, it is also important to him that he remain anonymous for fear of losing his high-level security clearance, which he relies on for his current and future employment. I can personally affirm that this individual is highly credible and had the assigned duties of targeting technician, assistant team chief at Malmstrom during this period.

On March 16, 1967, Smith was off duty when he was notified that the Echo sites had gone down and was directed to be part of a response team. The team he was dispatched with was *not* his day-to-day unit. It was simply two qualified personnel who could be contacted and "thrown together" for this impromptu scenario. His team was working on an Echo Flight LF that afternoon. By the time they had finished their checkout and were beginning their startup procedure, it was dark. The system went normal at first, up to the acquisition of the autocollimator light beam (an essential alignment of the guidance system inertial platform to provide a known geographical reference to relate to the desired launch azimuth for its target). At some point into this procedure, acquisition of the collimator failed. About this time, the topside security guard shook the ladder and motioned for Airman Smith to come up the ladder. When he reached ground level, he could see a large, glowing, orange-colored sphere, stationary at about thirty degrees from the horizon, in the direction of the gate and close to the site.

His first reaction was amazement, not fear of what he saw. The guard was shaken. Smith notified the team chief, who came up the ladder and also observed the object and became visibly shaken. At this point it became obvious to Airman Smith that due to his level of experience and calmer personality, he would have to assume de facto leadership of the operation. He ordered the guard to report this sighting to the Wing Command Post via the upstairs SIN (Sensitive Information Network) line. For some reason, the downstairs SIN line would not connect. In the meantime, Smith decided to return to his duties of bringing the missile back on Alert status. He and the other two members of the team tried the startup procedure several times. Each time the system reached the point of collimator acquisition it would "crap out." The object was still above the site.

During these attempts, Smith went up the ladder at times and noticed that the glow of the object would change to a pulsation of the light. He could feel the electrostatic energy around him. Moreover, he had the sense that the object was literally directing these pulses to a particular section of the ground operating equipment—the Guidance and Control System Coupler. This component translated the logic signals of the ground equipment to the operating voltage states of the guidance section computer. He could also hear a low-level hum as he felt the energy field from the object. However, he did not feel threatened by it. He concluded that he had no doubt the object "knew" a great deal about the most vulnerable part of the missile system and that it was demonstrating that it could indeed disable the missile at will!

The object was present for at least an hour; however, the guard told them later that it would periodically move away for a short time and then return. After considerably inhibiting the startup, it left the area; the missile was then brought back to Alert status with no anomalies whatever during collimator acquisition. Airman Smith said that neither the guard nor anybody on the team was observing the object at its time of departure. The guard later said that he had been watching it but became distracted by the VHF radio. When he looked up, it was simply gone.

Upon their return to Malmstrom early the next morning, the team was directed via VHF radio to proceed directly to the debriefing section. They were told not to make any other normal stops such as the base gas station to fuel up. Upon arriving at the 341st MIMS hangar, they were met inside by security personnel who accompanied them to debriefing. Upon arrival at debriefing the guard left with the security personnel and the targeting team was met by a lieutenant colonel (Smith does not recall his name) in dress (Class A blues) uniform whom Airman Smith clearly remembers as being fairly tall with graying hair and an "absolutely no-bullshit" attitude.

Before the debriefing, this lieutenant colonel directed the debriefing staff to leave the room. He then had the team debrief him on the incident. He showed no emotion during any of the discussions and was never confrontational, with one exception. When the targeting team chief started to give his version, it appeared to become obvious to the lieutenant colonel that the chief was not the one with the most knowledge of the operation, and he subsequently interacted primarily with Airman Smith during the remainder of the session. It was typical for the enlisted members, especially those with some experience, to be more competent at Launch Facility operations due to their much more in-depth training.

Smith could not remember any kind of recording device present, and also found it odd that the lieutenant colonel took no notes. Upon completion of the interview the lieutenant colonel directed that the events of that evening—not just observances of anything out of the ordinary, but also everything from the time of arrival to departure, the trip home, and up to and including this debriefing—was classified and could be discussed with no human being. Not among the team, the guard, the team's supervisor—nobody, period. He then thanked the team and directed the chief to go with him for additional discussions.

Airman Smith stated that, as directed, he never discussed this incident with anyone during his military career.

Now that the Echo incident has been declassified by the Air Force, it is important to him that the details of his incident are disclosed to the public. Through social contacts in the security group he was told that the guard was transferred to an overseas assignment the following week.

Because this incident was reported to the Wing Command Post, certainly Lieutenant Colonel Lewis Chase, the base operations officer, would have been informed about it. He would also have known about the Echo and Oscar incidents because of the intense pressure by Strategic Air Command (SAC) headquarters to find answers.

Also on the evening of March 24, 1967, a civilian truck driver, Ken Williams, observed a large, dome-shaped lighted object while driving near Belt, Montana (not far from Great Falls). The object was about a mile to his left and seemed to be pacing his truck at the same speed. Soon the object stopped and hovered for a moment, then dropped into a ravine and landed. Williams observed it as it pulsated with a very bright white light. This object was also seen by Bud Nader, a Montana Highway patrolman, before it left at high speed.

Chase was notified of this incident about an hour later because of all the UFO sighting reports coming into the base. After discussions with the base commander, Colonel Klibbe, he decided to investigate the situation. By 3:30 a.m., there had been numerous reports of sightings, including some over the Malmstrom base. That morning, details were put into a message sent to various Air Force offices, including the office of the Air Force Chief of Staff and the Foreign Technology Division at Wright-Patterson (TDET).

Great Falls Tribune Sunday, March 26, 1967

Staff Photo

I SAW THIS DOME-SHAPED LIGHT — Ken Williams, Laurel truck driver, explains to Carla Beck, Tribune staff writer, the appearance of an unidentified flying object he saw hovering near the top of Belt Hill Friday night. The interview was made at Belt Hill, where law enforcement officers, photographers and reporters gathered hoping to get a glimpse of the UFO.

UFO Breaks Monotony of Run

Report of the Belt Sighting in the *Great Falls Tribune*

Four months later, word had filtered back to TDET that there had been some equipment problems during the March 24 sightings. They sent an inquiry to Chase. It stated, "Our office has been informed that during the sightings there were equipment malfunctions and abnormalities in the equipment. One individual stated that the USAF instructed both military and civilian personnel not to discuss what they had seen as it was a classified government experiment. Request information on the validity of such statements. If some type of experiment did occur on or about 24 March 1967, please advise" (Monatt 1967).

Within a few days, Chase replied. "This office has no knowledge of equipment malfunctions and abnormalities in equipment during the period of reported UFO sightings. No validity can be established to the statement that a classified government experiment was in progress or that military and civilian personnel were requested not discuss what they had seen" (Chase 1967a).

These are blatantly false statements; I and others can attest that we were ordered not to talk to anyone about our incident and that our equipment certainly did malfunction. This written statement by Lieutenant Colonel Chase is clear evidence that he misrepresented the facts to the Foreign Technology Division (FTD) about all reports of UFOs disabling missiles.

This correspondence was written after the Condon Committee meeting with the Air Force Base UFO officers in June 1967. Because Chase was obviously not disclosing the missile shutdown incidents even to another Air Force office, clearly the cover-up was ongoing and he was in the middle of it. By the time Roy Craig came to ask questions about the Echo Flight incident, Chase would know what he was expected to do.

I was certainly not aware, at the time, of the ongoing Condon Committee Investigation. That intentionally bogus look at the UFO phenomena under USAF sponsorship, and how it responded to the Echo and Oscar incidents, is reviewed next.

THE NONSCIENTIFIC INVESTIGATION

In 1944, Edward U. Condon was a member of the Manhattan Project, which developed the first atomic bomb. He was removed from that project for unspecified reasons. In 1946, he was appointed to head the National Bureau of Standards (NBS). At that time, the NBS had responsibility for the Atomic Energy Commission (AEC). The AEC was in charge of all nuclear projects, including nuclear weapons testing. The NBS was also involved in classified weapons development projects—for example, the Kingfisher Project, a radar-controlled, air-launched torpedo for the Navy. In fact, the NBS was the model government agency for the implementation of new technologies in the development of cutting-edge military weaponry. An investigation stemming from allegations by FBI Director J. Edgar Hoover concluded that Condon was "nothing more or less than an espionage agent in disguise" (*Secrecy 1997*). Condon lost his security clearance in 1954.

In 1966, Condon was a professor of physics at the University of Colorado. According to Condon, that year he was contacted by someone from the Defense Department who suggested to him that it was time for him to seek reinstatement of his security clearance so that he could again work on government projects. Encouraged by this suggestion, Condon did apply and was granted reinstatement of his security clearance. Later that year, Condon was appointed chairman of the UFO study for the Air Force.

Soon after the Condon Committee began its work in earnest, the Air Force convened a meeting with the team at the University of Colorado on June 12, 1967. By this date, the Malmstrom UFO incidents had taken place, and Chase had been involved with the handling of those incidents. The Air Force had established special contacts for UFO matters at some of their bases. Those contacts, called Base UFO Investigators, were requested to attend this meeting by Major General Otto Glasser, assistant deputy chief of staff of the Air Force for research and development.

Chase held the highest ranking among these investigators, who were mostly junior grade officers. Chase wrote a trip report of this meeting and parts are quoted here. "Much effort was expended in explaining the methods that have been used to discount approximately 95 percent of the UFO sightings to date, i.e., optical mirage, stars, satellites, temperature inversion, etc. No time was devoted to the 5 percent of sightings on the Project Blue Book list that remain admittedly unexplained to date." In another paragraph, he stated: "It was also quite clear that, for the study to be effective, there is almost total dependency upon base UFO officers to sort the multitude of reports and to identify those cases worthy of detailed examination" (Chase 1967b).

Apparently the Air Force was going to be able to carefully control how they would be investigated. The last paragraph of Chase's trip report reveals much about how the Condon Committee and the Air Force were intending to orchestrate this program:

> *Although the university study has approximately eight months to run, and barring any dramatic events, the conclusions in the initial formal report will most likely read as*

follows: a) There is no evidence to support a hypothesis that extraterrestrials have visited Earth. b) Certain events have occurred that are difficult to explain due to lack of conclusive data and/or instrumentation and state-of-the-art investigative procedures. (Chase 1967b)

He concluded by saying, "However, it is reemphasized that there will be no big change in the UFO program, unless it is a civilian/military sharing of charges of concealing information from the public" (Chase 1967b). Because Chase was the highest-ranking officer at this meeting, he was effectively representing the Air Force brass. He had been directed to attend the meeting by a major general at the highest levels of Air Force headquarters. And with his trip report, he was prepared to respond to any inquiries from headquarters about the meeting and whether or not the Condon Committee would cooperate in the manner the Air Force desired. It seems that those questions were answered for him.

On August 9, 1967, Dr. Roy Craig made a visit to the home of Raymond Fowler to discuss some reports of sightings that might be beneficial for review by the Condon investigation. Craig was part of the US Air Force–financed University of Colorado UFO Study Group chaired by Dr. Condon (the Condon Committee). Fowler had been assigned the title of "Early Warning Coordinator" for the group by virtue of the fact that he was an investigator for National Investigations Committee on Aerial Phenomena (NICAP). He was also on the Sylvania Minuteman Production board in support of their contract with the Air Force for the Minuteman Missile ground electrical systems.

Fowler had received field reports of missile equipment failures at missile sites in Montana. He specifically told Craig about the reports he had received from sources on site that these failures were associated with the appearance of UFOs around the missile sites. Craig was of course obligated to take these reports seriously because he was assigned as a principal investigator to look into such incidents as part of the study.

DR. ROY CRAIG

Craig received his PhD in physical chemistry. In 1966, he was an associate professor at the University of Colorado when the university was awarded $500,000 by the Air Force to do a scientific study on the UFO phenomenon. Craig had no experience or training in investigative procedures and, by his own admission, only had a passing interest in UFOs. He knew little of the history of the phenomenon when he began working with the group. Yet he was assigned as one of three principal investigators for the study. "My assignment would be to investigate the physical aspects of current UFO reports, working with a staff psychologist, who would study the psychological aspects of the report. . . . My associate would look into the minds of the persons reporting the sightings" (Craig 1995, xx).

Even before looking into cases, Craig was tasked to work with a psychologist. The clear implication here is that the group leadership had a predisposition to think that the reports of UFOs could be explained as delusions of the mind. In fact, Condon had assigned no fewer than three psychologists to work with the investigators. In addition, Craig had stipulated to Condon that he would accept the assignment if he did not have to deal with any classified information. "If an investigation led to a requirement for access to secret information, which seldom happened, I turned the case over to another member of the project and accepted his judgment regarding the extent of UFO pertinence to the case" (Craig 1995, 170–171).

As the group was organized, Condon deputy Robert Low was the only member who was authorized to review classified material. That was problematic from the beginning of the study. In August 1966, prior to the start of the study, Low had written a memo to university officials stating in part:

> Our study would be conducted almost exclusively by non-believers who, although they couldn't possibly prove a negative result, could and probably would add an impressive body of evidence that there is no reality to the observations. The trick would be, I think, to describe the project so that, to the public, it would appear a totally objective study but, to the scientific community, would present the image of a group of nonbelievers trying their best to be objective, but having an almost zero expectation of finding a saucer. One way to do this would be to stress investigation, not of the physical phenomena, but rather of the people who do the observing—the psychology and sociology of persons and groups who report seeing UFOs. If the emphasis were put here, rather than on examination of the old question of the physical reality of the saucer, I think the scientific community would quickly get the message. . . . I'm inclined to feel at this early stage that, if we set up the thing right and take pains to get the proper people involved and have success in presenting the image we want to present to the scientific community, we could carry the job off to our benefit. (Low 1966)

Low was outlining a plan whereby they could not only get the Air Force off the hook on UFOs but also give the scientific community every excuse not to get involved. When it counted the most, Low would fail to push the Air Force for the release of information on a classified investigation that very much involved UFOs and national security.

A VISIT TO MALMSTROM AIR FORCE BASE (OCTOBER 9–14, 1967)

According to his own notes, written during his visit to Malmstrom, Craig had specific objectives for this visit. He wanted to review with Lieutenant Colonel Lewis Chase his own UFO encounter in 1957 while flying a training mission as aircraft commander of an RB-47. In addition, he wanted to look into the reports of UFOs during missile shutdowns. He also wanted to interview witnesses to the 1950 Nick Mariana incident during which UFOs were filmed flying over Great Falls, Montana.

Craig knew of the UFO-related shutdowns at missile sites from Ray Fowler (NICAP) and was given the names of specific individuals to interview. It is significant that he notes, more than once, the date of the shutdowns as March 24, 1967. We note that civilian contractors for Minuteman, such as Sylvania and Boeing, were warned not to talk about the incidents. In fact, Fowler admits that he only mentioned the rumors of the Echo Flight shutdown of ten Minuteman missiles to Craig with some trepidation about losing his job and security clearance. The report of the shutdowns was cloaked in secrecy even before Craig arrived at Malmstrom. The depth of that secrecy would soon be escalated after his arrival.

In Craig's book regarding his experience with the Condon Committee, he describes his encounter with Chase:

> *After Colonel Chase and I had exchanged pleasantries in his office, I asked him about the Echo incident. The colonel caught his breath, and expressed surprise that I knew of it. "I can't talk about that.". . . . If I needed to know the cause of this incident, I could arrange through official channels, to see their report after completion of the investigation. . . . Although local newspapers carried stories of UFO sightings, which would coincide in time with Echo, Colonel Chase had assured me that the incident had not involved a UFO. . . . I accepted the information as factual and turned review of Major Schraff's report [on the Echo Incident] over to Bob Low, who had received security clearance to read secret information related to the UFO study. (Craig 1995, 171–172)*

From our research on local news reports of UFO sightings, we could not find any relevant newspaper articles around the 16th or 17th of March, 1967. The *Great Falls Tribune* did, however, have multiple stories about the UFO sightings that occurred on the 24th of March, the time of the Oscar shutdowns. When Craig spoke with Chase about the Echo Flight incident, he was under the impression that it had occurred on the 24th because that was the date given to him by Fowler. Neither of them had realized at the time there were two separate incidents on different dates.

Robert Low was required to interface with his Air Force liaison, Colonel Hippler, in Washington. Craig wrote a memo to Low suggesting he ask Hippler for the

Echo Flight investigation report. Low's note at the bottom of this handwritten memo states: "Roy, I called Hippler and he said he would try to get this, but he suspects it's going to be classified too high for us to look at it. Says he thinks interference by pulses from nuclear explosions (testing) is probably involved."

The tone of this note indicates that Low was simply accepting this rationale for classifying the missile shutdowns as a non-UFO event. According to records of Dr. James McDonald, Robert Low never followed up on this request. If Low had followed up on his request and asked for more details, such as asking the Air Force for more information about the possibility of nuclear explosion EMP impacting just two flights of missiles, he might have discovered that the United States did not test any nuclear weapons in the period from March 10 through April 4, 1967, the time period of the shutdowns (USDOE 2000).

Even on the face of it, Low should have realized that if nuclear EMP were truly the cause for the shutdowns, it would have created widespread havoc throughout our strategic missile forces. Clearly the reasons given by Hippler were irrational and simply intended to give cover to Low and others to back away from any further investigation by the Condon Committee of the Malmstrom missile shutdowns.

Craig's notes indicate that he knew the names of many individuals whom he could have interviewed with respect to "rumors" of UFO involvement in the missile shutdowns. Fowler had given Craig the names of civilian representatives from Sylvania and Boeing who had first-hand knowledge of the UFO sightings. Fowler also gave

Craig the name of a member of the Site Activation Task Force (SATAF) who was a very credible eyewitness. He reported being within a few feet of the object. In addition, one of the NCOs on the Air Force Technical Evaluation team admitted to seeing an object. There is no record of Craig interviewing these men. Craig did not ask to know the names of any of the Echo/Oscar Flight crews on duty at the time of the shutdowns, or any maintenance or security personnel at Echo.

It should be noted that Walter Figel, the deputy missile combat crew commander (DMCCC) of Echo Flight during its UFO encounter, was sent to Strategic Air Command (SAC) headquarters to debrief their commander about the incident soon after it occurred. A *secret* telex (dated March 17, 1967; declassified under FOIA January 16, 1996) sent from SAC headquarters clearly expressed the "grave concern" of SAC and the need to find answers "as quickly as possible." Hank Barlow, a maintenance crew chief who worked on the Echo Flight soon after the incident, reported seeing a lot of brass from Offutt Air Force Base (SAC HQ) at Echo LCF and was told about UFO involvement in the shutdowns.

The 341st Missile Wing history report covering the period of the shutdowns reported the following with respect to the ongoing investigation of Echo Flight: "The opinion of the team was that external generated signals caused the generation of these two channels and shutdown of the launch facilities. The possibility of this is very remote due to the fact that all 10 couplers would have to fail in the flight within a few seconds of each other" (Gamble 1967, 37).

The fact that missiles had been disabled during encounters with UFOs was clearly known to SAC headquarters and higher. And yet, the Air Force-sponsored Condon Study was intentionally kept in the dark about it.

It is also important to emphasize that, although Craig was charged with investigating these incidents, by his own admission, he simply took the word of Chase that there was no UFO involvement, and did not pursue an in-depth investigation as he was authorized to do and was supposed to do.

In August 1966, Lieutenant Colonel Robert Hippler, representing the Air Force Office of Science and Technology and serving as the study group's contact with the Pentagon, stood before the highly educated group Edward Condon had selected to participate in the study and told them that they had not been charged with proving or disproving anything about the UFO phenomenon.

He may not have realized it, but he was telling his audience not to perform a scientific study. The scientific method is understood by anyone who has ever passed a science class in high school. A scientific method consists of the collection of data through observation and experimentation, and the formulation and testing of hypotheses relative to that data. By its own admission, the Air Force did not give the study group any hypothesis to prove or disprove. It did not provide the group with all the data it had in its possession or access to witnesses. In fact, the Air Force had classified UFO files and reports that were not made available to the study group. Thus, the scientific method could not have been used.

The Air Force did not really want the scientific study it had promised Congress and the public. It simply wanted to divest itself of the responsibility of responding to public inquiry on the subject of UFOs.

Dr. James McDonald, who had investigated sightings throughout the United States and in Australia, had provided the study group with a list of twenty best cases. The study group declined to look at them.

As Lieutenant Colonel Chase had pointed out, it would be up to the Air Force to decide which cases ought to be investigated. And, although Blue Book opened up their files to the group, the classified cases were not made available for investigation. Chase lied to Craig about UFO involvement in the Echo incident and did not mention the fact that on March 24, Oscar Flight was also shut down by UFOs. Craig was told that Echo Flight was disabled on the 24th, and that was never corrected (the actual date was March 16) by anyone in the Air Force because then they would have had to admit that a second flight (Oscar) was disabled under similar circumstances.

Roy Craig had refused to look at any cases that might involve a security classification. He simply bought into Chase's explanation and did no further investigation of an incident that was referred to him by credible sources. Therefore, one of the most important incidents related to UFOs, the Malmstrom missile shutdowns, which could have had a major impact on the results of the study, was not even considered in the final analysis.

As has been stated before, the Condon study was simply a whitewash of the UFO "problem," and that paint job was bought and paid for by the Air Force. This was a critical period in time on the question of public disclosure of information held by our government about the phenomenon. As a result of the "findings" of the Condon study, the Air Force took and has ever since taken the position that the phenomenon has no bearing on our national security interest and therefore no relevance to the Air Force or any other government agency. Therefore, they claim, they no longer investigate UFO reports. This policy has, of course, allowed the withholding of facts and information from the public to continue. It has allowed the making of policies and government intervention with and about these unknown objects without oversight, public discourse, or approval. It has allowed an intolerable abuse of secrecy by our government.

Capt. Robert L. Salas. Official USAF photo.

On March 26, 1967, I woke up groggy from my twenty-four-hour "tour in the hole," as we referred to duty in the underground capsule. As I recall, that morning I picked up the *Great Falls Tribune* and read accounts of UFO reports around the area. Later that afternoon, I received a call from one of the airmen who had seen the object at Oscar Flight where we had experienced the strange incident the morning before. He pleaded with—no, begged—me to meet with him to talk about what had happened. All he wanted to do was talk about it. He had been one of the security guards who had to stand in abject terror in front of this large, red, pulsating ball of light by our front gate with only a rifle in his hands. He told me unashamedly that he was confused and frightened by what he had seen and he was desperate to speak with me about it. I had to tell him that I had taken an oath not to speak about the incident to anyone and could not meet with him.

As much as anything that has transpired in my life, that conversation has consistently haunted me to this day. I was unaware at that time that the entire flight of ten Minuteman missiles was also disabled while UFOs were observed over the launch facilities of Echo Flight on March 16, 1967. Those crews, too, were not allowed to talk about it. James Klotz and I have documented these events in our book, *Faded Giant*. There are multiple, credible witness statements and documentation to support these claims. I feel I have an obligation to that airman I spoke with, to all the other officers and men in the Air Force who have had to keep silent, and to those who have come forward with what they experienced with these objects. The body of the evidence to support the truth of these incidents includes documents and witness testimonies that have been duly sworn to and/or stated publicly. Therefore, I, without reservation, accuse the US Department of the Air Force of a blatant, pervasive, and continuing cover-up of the facts; deception; distortion; and lying to the public about the reality of the UFO phenomenon.

ADDENDUM — OCTOBER 2022

Col. (ret.) Walter Figel was the Deputy Missile Combat Crew Commander (DMCCC) of Echo Launch Control Facility (LCF) when the incident occurred on March 16, 1967. He has given multiple statements about the events to myself and researcher Robert Hastings. These statements have been recorded on audio tape with his permission. He was in command of the Echo LCF at the time of the incident.

Summarizing his statements, Col. Figel confirmed the following: There were maintenance personnel and security guards at the Launch Facility (LF) that was the first to shut down. All of them reported seeing the UFO overhead when this occurred. He recalls that LCF security guards were sent out to investigate the LFs, not knowing about the UFOs, and they reported seeing them.

Upon their return to Malmstrom, both of the crew members, Eric Carlson and Walter Figel, reported to their squadron commander and were debriefed. Figel recalls that he and Carlson debriefed higher-ranking officers from Strategic Air Command Headquarters on the incident. Figel stated that he was even flown to Offutt AFB in Nebraska to give his debriefing of the incident. They were told not speak about their incident to anyone. After I spoke with Col. Figel in 1996, I gave him the phone number and address of Eric Carlson. In a letter to me, Carlson confirmed what Figel had told me during our initial conversation (see below).

During my investigation into the two incidents, I received letters from other airmen who confirmed various aspects of the incidents. For example, I received a letter from a member of a maintenance team that was assigned to bring some of the Echo flight missiles back on Alert status. He stated, "At that time, half of Echo was down; by the time we got there the rest of the flight was down. We started up at least 3 birds that morning and had to stay at Echo 1 [Launch Control Facility] that night. A lot of brass was there and there was no place to lay down."

Another letter from an airman knowledgeable of the Oscar incident stated, "[T]he security guard that Captain Salas spoke about that had to be helicoptered to the base hospital created quite a stir back at the barracks. It is my understanding that he aimed his weapon at the craft and I heard both ways that he did discharge his weapon and was knocked to the ground or attempted to discharge his weapon and was rendered unconscious and I believe had also a hand injury."

As part of their investigation, Boeing engineers performed a bench test on a piece of the hardware called the logic coupler used in the Minuteman guidance system in an attempt to isolate the failure mode. They were able to cause an interruption in the logic coupler by injecting an electrical signal of a certain frequency and duration that would cause the system to shut down. However, they were unable to determine how such a signal could be inserted into each of the ten missile logic couplers within seconds of each other. They concluded that the probability of that happening was extremely remote.

In order to insert a specific signal such as the one described into a missile system remotely, the object observed over the LCF would have had to send the signal through sixty feet of earth and reinforced concrete, penetrate a triple-shielded cable, and direct it to a specific piece of hardware (the logic coupler) for each of the ten missiles within seconds of one another. I challenge anyone to identify any manmade device that could have performed that task in 1967—or even today.

CHAPTER 3

Extreme Secrecy

*"A popular government without popular information,
or the means of acquiring it, is but a prologue to a farce
or a tragedy or perhaps both. Knowledge will forever
govern ignorance; and the people who mean to be their
own governors must arm themselves with the power,
which knowledge gives. "*

—JAMES MADISON, "FATHER OF THE
US CONSTITUTION"

Ever since I can remember, America has seemed to always
be on a "war" footing. I remember, at age four, sitting by
the radio with my sister, listening to President Roosevelt
talking about the wars in the Pacific and Europe. My fifth-
grade teacher told us stories about his experiences in the
war in Korea. As a teenager, we were told there would be
"fallout shelters" located and identified in urban settings
across the nation, preparing the civilian population for a
nuclear war. In school we learned how to "duck" under
desks. Of course, the enormity of these bombs would be
much larger than we could survive. By then, not known to
the public, the hydrogen bomb, a thousand times more
powerful than the Hiroshima bomb, had been produced

by the USSR and the United States. The real facts of nuclear weapons and the probabilities of nuclear war were official secrets withheld from the public. This was one dilemma of the Cold War. To preserve an open society it was deemed necessary to take measures that in significant ways closed it down. A culture of greater secrecy evolved.

In a conflict between the right to know and the need to protect true military secrets from a potential enemy, there can be no valid argument against secrecy. The right to know has suffered, however, in the confusion of the demarcation between secrecy for true security reasons and secrecy for "policy" reasons. The proper imposition of secrecy in some situations is a matter of judgment. Although an official faces disciplinary action for the failure to classify information that should be secret, no instance has been found of an official facing disciplinary or criminal action for classifying material that should have been made public. The tendency to "play it safe" and use the secrecy stamp has, therefore, been virtually the norm.

SECRECY IN GOVERNMENT

Though it is acknowledged that national governments must have the ability to keep secrets in order to protect their nation's security, there is a propensity by government to overindulge in secrecy and therefore deny the public the knowledge needed to engage government on particular issues. Here in the United States, this excessive secrecy has been ongoing for such a long period of time that many abuses by various government agencies have degraded and continue to degrade the cornerstone of our democratic principles—government of, by, and for the people.

According to Dr. Jeffrey Richelson, a specialist in intelligence activities:

> *The U.S. Intelligence community consists of seventeen organizations: the Office of the Director of National Intelligence, the Central Intelligence Agency, the National Security Agency, the National Reconnaissance Office, the National Geospatial Intelligence Agency, the Defense Intelligence Agency, the Bureau of Intelligence and Research of the State Department, the intelligence elements of the five military services, the Federal Bureau of Investigation, and intelligence components of the Drug Enforcement Administration, the Department of Energy, the Department of the Treasury, and the Department of Homeland Security. (Richelson 2016, 13)*

Although these agencies are under the executive branch, they are also supposed to be under the oversight of the Congress. In reality, that oversight is practically nonexistent.

In 2004, I attended a reunion of my USAF Academy class of 1964. During one of the events of that reunion, one of my classmates spoke to us about his involvement with a Special Access Program (SAP). SAPs, commonly referred to as "black projects," are programs that involve extra security and a finite list of people who are authorized access to the classified information. Although congressional intelligence committees are required to be briefed on their activities, there are very few detailed briefings given to committees about these programs. My classmate confirmed this, saying how easy it was to simply brief them on his program with superficial and superfluous details.

The rationale used by these agencies to classify information is that public release of the information would harm our national security. The application of the principle of some information being vital to our national security is, at its core, a judgment call. Normally the reasons for making the decision to classify do not have to be justified, unless challenged in court. That rarely happens. Therefore, information is classified unnecessarily as a precaution to the possibility that it might somehow impact our national security interests. In addition, many times material is classified to avoid public disclosure of mistakes by an agency or for political expediency or to hide illegal actions such as the Iran-Contra affair or CIA rendition and torture activities.

THE STATE OF THE UNION OF SECRECY

President Obama declared his intention to have a more open government and allow the declassification of material that is inappropriately classified. His policy, as documented in a memorandum to the heads of executive departments and agencies on January 21, 2009, states, in part:

> In our democracy, the Freedom of Information Act (FOIA), which encourages accountability through transparency, is the most prominent expression of a profound national commitment to ensuring an open Government. At the heart of that commitment is the idea that accountability is in the interest of the Government and the citizenry alike.

> The Freedom of Information Act should be administered with a clear presumption: In the face of doubt, openness prevails. The Government should not keep information

*confidential merely because public officials might be embar-
rassed by disclosure, because errors and failures might be
revealed, or because of speculative or abstract fears. (The
White House 2009)*

This policy statement was followed by an executive
order in May 2009 that directed each executive department and agency to recommend improvements on
their handling of classified material. It also directed the
establishment of a National Declassification Center to
coordinate the efforts of the various agencies in their
declassification review.

Because this new policy and directive are essentially
requiring all government agencies to air their "dirty
laundry" with respect to classified material, I think the
response will vary from foot-dragging to outright attempts
to avoid implementing this policy. Government agencies
are miniempires that are generally controlled by career
bureaucrats. The classification of material for any reason
has been inbred for so long that it will probably take a
great effort to change that culture.

In 2011, the American Civil Liberties Union (ACLU)
issued its report on US secrecy laws and oversight of the
security establishment. That report emphasizes the critical issues involving extreme secrecy within the federal
government. The report states that in 2009 there were
an estimated 2.4 million Defense Department civilian,
military, and contractor personnel holding security clearances at various levels. According to a 2010 report by
the Information Security Oversight Office (ISOO), the
government made 76.8 million classification decisions,
a more than 40 percent increase from 2009. The cost of

security classification activities alone cost the executive branch $10.2 billion in 2010.

In 2013, the Federation of American Scientists (FAS), along with twenty-nine other concerned organizations, stated that excesses in secrecy had become uncontrollable and called for greater oversight at the executive level. The letter to the President stated:

> As you know, the national security classification system sweeps in far too much information that should actually be available to the public, creating unnecessary barriers to public deliberation on many policy issues in counterterrorism, intelligence policy, and the conduct of foreign affairs. As public frustration over unjustified secrecy mounts, respect for the security classification system plummets, placing genuinely sensitive information at risk. Yet up to now, no constructive resolution of this impasse has emerged.
>
> In principle, classification authority should be used with precision and only when absolutely necessary to protect the security of the United States. In practice, however, classification activity has been dramatically on the rise for many years, with over 92 million decisions to classify information in fiscal year 2011 alone. Declassification procedures cannot possibly keep pace, especially given the legal and bureaucratic obstacles to declassification that currently exist. This approach is unsustainable and counterproductive. (FAS et al. 2013, 1)

SECRET SCIENCE

In July 2012, the Congressional Research Service published a report titled "Publishing Scientific Papers with Potential Security Risks: Issues for Congress." This report identifies the problems associated with publishing results of federally funded research studies that could have "dual uses." It states that some of the uses of this kind of research could be for malicious purposes:

> *The current issues under debate cut across traditional policy areas, involving simultaneous consideration of security, scientific, health, export and international policy. Because of the complexity of these issues, analysis according to one set of policy priorities may adversely affect other policy priorities. For example, maximizing security may lead to detriments in public health and scientific advancement, while maximizing scientific advancement may lead to security risks. Accounting for such trade-offs may allow policymakers to establish regulatory frameworks that more effectively maximize the benefits from "dual-use" . . . research while mitigating its potential risks. (Gottron and Shea 2013, ii)*

What it does not state is that congressional inaction in this area, the most likely scenario, would result in the continued security classification of these scientific studies, thereby making them unavailable to the public.

The main allure of secrecy in politics may be the influence of power in government that it brings. Holding a secret has always been a way of having some sort of power over others. However, if that power is misused and that misuse is perpetuated through acceptance of practices, the excesses of secrecy in government will ultimately hurt us all because informed decision-making has been weakened.

For example, in 1995 a group of scientists proposed the idea of gaining access to some of the reservoir of data collected by spy satellites so that it could be put to good use in scientific research (Richelson 1998, 48–55). This idea led to the formation of a group called Medea, consisting of dozens of scientists who had been granted high-level security clearances. Medea reviewed this plethora of data to determine if it could be used to study trends in global warming, ocean temperatures, vegetation and forest cover, the spread of deserts, and other environmental issues. However, problems associated with dissemination of this classified data quickly arose.

The article points out that science is based on two important pillars:

1. The ability of one scientist to reproduce another's findings by using the same data, and

2. The ability to demonstrate the validity of the findings through experimentation or observation.

The use of classified data to establish a scientific hypothesis eliminates the first pillar. The use of classified data also eliminates the ability to peer-review the analysis. As a result, the use of classified data by civilian agencies could inhibit free and open discussion of some policies.

In 2009, Medea persuaded intelligence officials to publicly share images of areas of environmental interest that had, by that time, been photographed regularly for more than a decade. The images are now archived as the Global Fiducials Library, available through the US Geological Survey (USGS). The data are invaluable because they are gathered roughly once every few weeks—more frequently and continuously than those from civilian research satellites.

Lindley Johnson, who oversees NASA's Near-Earth Object Observation program, believes that the space policy unveiled in 2010 by President Barack Obama, which explicitly endorses data sharing, may have smoothed his efforts to secure data from the US Air Force. Johnson says the new arrangement, which will give astronomers access to data from missile-warning satellites on all meteors—not just the ones researchers knew about already—will allow scientists to gain a better understanding of the range of near-Earth objects in orbit.

How much science will emerge from these burgeoning relationships remains to be seen. So far, the image libraries of the Arctic and Antarctic have seen only modest use from scientists. "One of our biggest challenges is to educate the science community about the existence of our program" (Brumfiel 2011, 388–389), says Bruce Molnia, executive director of the Civil Applications Committee at the USGS in Reston, Virginia, which oversees civilian use of classified image data. The members of Medea, who have access to the full array of classified data, are—for now at least—using it to address policy questions raised by government agencies, such as what national security risks are posed by climate change, rather than conducting fundamental research of their own choosing.

THE STATE SECRETS PRIVILEGE

The following is quoted directly from a Congressional Research Service report:

The state secrets privilege is a judicially created evidentiary privilege that allows the federal government to resist court-ordered disclosure of information during litigation if there is a reasonable danger that such disclosure would harm the national security of the United States.

Although the common law privilege has a long history, the Supreme Court first described the modern analytical framework of the state secrets privilege in the 1953 case of United States v. Reynolds, 345 U.S. 1 (1953). In Reynolds, the court laid out a two-step procedure to be used when evaluating a claim of privilege to protect state secrets. First, there must be a formal claim of privilege, lodged by the head of the department that has control over the matter, after actual, personal consideration by that officer. Second, a court must independently determine whether the circumstances are appropriate for the claim of privilege, and yet do so without forcing a disclosure of the very matter the privilege is designed to protect. If the privilege is appropriately invoked, it is an absolute, and the disclosure of the underlying information cannot be compelled [or] released by a court. A valid invocation of the privilege does not necessarily require dismissal of the claim. In Reynolds, for instance, the Supreme Court did not dismiss the plaintiffs' claims, but rather remanded the case to determine whether the claims could proceed absent the privileged evidence. Yet, significant controversy has arisen with respect to the question of how a case should proceed in light of a successful claim of privilege.

Courts have varied greatly in their willingness to either grant government motions to dismiss a claim in its entirety or allow a case to proceed "with no consequences save those resulting from the loss of evidence." Some courts have taken a more restrained view of the consequences of a valid privilege, holding that the privilege protects only specific pieces of privileged evidence. In contrast, other courts have taken a more expansive view, arguing that the privilege, with its constitutional underpinnings, often requires deference to executive branch assertions, and ultimately leaves a party with no other available remedy. . . . Most recently, in May of 2011, the Supreme Court held that the valid invocation of

> *the state secrets privilege could render a defense contracting*
> *dispute non-justiciable, leaving both the defense contractor*
> *and the Pentagon without any judicial remedies to enforce*
> *the contract. (CRS 2011)*

It is easy to draw the conclusion that public disclosure of the UFO phenomenon will never happen because of the extensive, exhaustive secrecy bureaucracy and the compartmentalization of information on the subject. I think the real issue is not how and if it will happen. The importance of the disclosure question is that it must happen to preserve our democracy.

UFO DISCLOSURE AS A ZERO-SUM GAME

In 1944, mathematicians John von Neumann and Oskar Morgenstern published a book on the theory of games. One premise of this book was that mathematics could be applied to the study of social relations in the form of a game. It was not intended to oversimplify complex social interactions but an attempt to analyze relatively simple aspects of that interaction.

One concept that was introduced in the book was the zero-sum game. A zero-sum game is one in which the sum of all payoffs in the game is zero. For example, if one player wins a point, the other player loses a point. The total number of points available to win or lose does not change, and therefore the net sum of those points is always the same: zero. The interaction of the players or the play of the game results in a differential of points, but the sum remains zero. Each payoff (or point) is considered to have some utility (benefit) to a player. Utilities can be perceived as large or small advantages depending on how much information a player has about the other's strategies. If a game is played well, both players are using a rational strategy to minimize losing large point utilities to their opponent. If the game is played with an optimum strategy by both players, the game is said to be in equilibrium. That does not mean that neither player is winning; it means the point difference is staying, relatively, the same.

The ongoing attempt we have been making to get government disclosure of the UFO phenomenon could be viewed as a social game as just described. As long as there is no public disclosure about the UFO reality, the game goes on and there are no absolute winners or losers. You could say we are in a state of equilibrium in this game.

As in all games there are risks. In the disclosure game, the government is risking some loss in the public trust (low risk, minimal consequences because the public expects not to trust the government). On the public's side, we risk ridicule, loss of job opportunities, and our reputations (high risk, maximum consequences). Because of the imbalance of these opposing risk factors, the government has a significant advantage in this game. However, it may be worthwhile to take a closer look at this game in the context of a historical perspective and to check the effectiveness of strategies.

Let us suppose that there is a secret organizational structure, a cabal, within our government that is holding the cache of UFO-related information. Let us also suppose that we form a cohesive group of people dedicated to disclosure. Let us make the further leap of faith that we are working in concert and have drawn the same conclusions about the phenomenon and the cabal. Then, we might consider this a game in play between two players.

Each side has some tactics available to use in this game. These can be applied as are moves in a game of chess. Effective tactics for us might include: obtaining and publicizing credible witness testimony and documents, conducting investigations of incidents, engaging the media in serious discussions, rigorous review of historical records, and performing scientific analyses of potential artifacts. Effective tactics for the cabal might include: operating a disinformation campaign, providing plausible explanations of incidents, maintaining silence on incidents, infiltrating UFO groups to disrupt or gain information, intimidating witnesses, and promoting ridicule. The planning and execution for the use of these tactics would constitute an effective strategy. The optimum strategy for each side will be revealed during the play of the game.

Let us say the two sides have been playing this game since the Roswell incident in 1947. The cabal may have had their origins as a result of that incident, because by deciding to lie about it, they established a need for withholding the truth of the details of such events from the public. Their initial tactics were to maintain a high level of secrecy through intimidation of witnesses and to compartmentalize the information to a select few. The public was given a false "cover" story to provide plausible deniability. The tactics used: disinformation, intimidation, and silence. Our side may have joined the game a few weeks earlier with the sighting of a "flying saucer" shaped craft by Kenneth Arnold over Mt. Rainier in Washington.

With these two initial major UFO events, the public became interested in the possibility of alien visitors again. This was not some fear-based interest like the "alien scare" of 1938 from the misunderstood radio broadcast of *The War of the Worlds* by H. G. Wells but genuine curiosity. Then, some years later, there was another major sighting by thousands of people over Washington, DC! Subsequently, UFO interest groups such as Aerial Phenomenon Research Organization (APRO) and National Investigations Committee on Aerial Phenomena (NICAP) began forming to seriously investigate the phenomenon. Our tactics: attempting to acquire and verify information and to document these UFO cases.

The cabal had the advantage in this game from the beginning. Assuming they had recovered actual craft and bodies of ETs, which is a fair assumption, they had definitive evidence of this reality. More importantly, they had the experience and the means to run highly secretive operations. The US government had just successfully completed one of the most extensive and complex secret projects in history: the development and delivery of the first atomic bomb. The year 1947 was also when the CIA was established as the key intelligence organ of the government. The CIA was staffed with highly experienced OSS agents from World War II. They knew how to maintain secrets, the art of disinformation, spying and coercion of witnesses, and how to command and control a complex clandestine network.

Initially, our side struggled just to make sense of the occasional UFO reports that would be reported in the paper or by other witnesses with the courage to come forward. Very quickly, however, the phenomenon became the subject of ridicule or science fiction movies. It was easier for the public to make light of the rumored sightings and visits by "little green men" than to take it seriously. But after the mass sightings in 1952, our government was forced to take a more serious stance on the subject.

The Robertson Panel, instigated by the CIA, was convened in secret in 1953 to look into the UFO question. The result of this panel's "investigation" was to initiate a disinformation campaign. The Air Force officially established Project Sign to take reports of the phenomenon, and followed that with Project Grudge and then Project Blue Book. What neither side in this game could predict was what sighting or event would happen next. In the early 1960s, the Betty and Barney Hill abduction case became known. After that, more witnesses came forward with their own accounts of alien abduction. We were being helped by more credible reports, but the cabal countered with more disinformation and ridicule.

In March 1966, near Dexter, Michigan, a number of police officers and radar operators at Selfridge Air Force Base observed four UFOs. This mass sighting led to a clamor for a government investigation of the incident. Congressman Gerald Ford called for an investigation of the entire UFO phenomenon. Within months, the Air Force agreed to have an independent body conduct a "scientific" investigation. In August 1966, the University of Colorado was awarded $500,000 to conduct this investigation. This would prove to be another example of cabal tactics of deception and disinformation. I have previously documented the deliberate deception of the Condon Committee. It was not a scientific investigation; it was a preplanned sham set up by the Air Force to provide an excuse to officially declare an end to their investigations of UFO sightings.

Without official reports, we were left to our own efforts to try to investigate UFO sightings. Some of these reports seemed fantastic to the public, whereas others were invented by the cabal in order to promote skepticism. In addition, the aspect of the phenomenon of abductions seemed to become more pronounced during the 1980s and 1990s as more witnesses came forward. As a result, the public and media perception of the phenomenon again leaned toward ridicule and disbelief.

However, in 1978, through the efforts of Mr. Stanton Friedman, a very key witness came forward. Retired Air Force Major Jesse Marcel, an intelligence officer at Roswell Army Air Base in 1947, disclosed that what was recovered near the base was indeed the crashed remains of an extraterrestrial craft and alien bodies. From this initial disclosure and from further investigative efforts, hundreds of witnesses came forward to validate the truth of the event. So much public interest resulted from these reports that the Air Force found it necessary to revisit the incident with their own "investigation."

In 1994, they issued a report stating that they verified that the crashed debris was simply that of a weather balloon. In 1995, they amended that story and claimed that the balloon was actually used as a vehicle for spying on the Soviet nuclear program. However, this time, the public as a whole did not fully buy the Air Force story. Much has been written and discussed about the Roswell case, and it is safe to say most people think it did happen according to the accounts of witnesses.

In 1997, hundreds of people reported seeing a huge object silently flying over Phoenix, Arizona. The witnesses to this event include the ex-governor of the state. To date, this sighting has not been credibly challenged by the government.

In 2001, a large group of civilian and ex-military witnesses held a press conference in Washington, DC, disclosing more credible reports of UFO encounters. I am proud to say I was one of those witnesses. Again, none of these disclosures were or have been plausibly challenged by our government.

In 2007 and again in 2010, more ex-military witnesses, including some from other countries, came together at public press conferences to disclose UFO encounters at military bases. More recently, in April 2013, the Citizen's Hearing on Disclosure was held in Washington, DC. This was a mock congressional hearing that included five ex-congressmen and women and one ex-senator. The compelling testimony and the quality of the witnesses convinced each of them that the UFO phenomenon deserves a real congressional hearing.

Today, the cabal and those of us trying to challenge it are still engaged in this zero-sum game. Although the cabal continues to use the tactics of silence, ridicule, disinformation, and media control, it could be argued that they are becoming less effective in the battle for public opinion. Silence in the face of mounting evidence by the accounts of credible witnesses to the reality of the phenomenon cannot remain a viable government response indefinitely. The intimidation of witnesses through ridicule and other means can only remain effective if the more-questionable or superficial UFO encounter stories are publicized and speculative opinions and unsupported claims are voiced. These misguided activities make it easier for the media to promote the ridicule that has haunted the accurate reporting on the subject. Alternately, if we promote those cases that have been well documented and verified through multiple witnesses, our side will keep our momentum in this game. In addition, we can anticipate more witnesses coming forward in the future.

Clearly there is a coverup of the UFO phenomenon, and clearly the forces in favor of disclosure are at a disadvantage in winning this game. The prize is the entire pie. We want total disclosure and the other side wants to keep the facts completely hidden. Even if we assume that the other side has the good intention of keeping the public ignorant of these facts so that they will not be frightened or dismayed about what is actually taking place, it is still a small group of individuals making very important decisions for the entire human population. That is simply not right by any standard.

DISCLOSURE

The so-called "disclosure movement" efforts by some groups have, apparently, the same objective: to discover what the government knows about the UFO phenomenon. However, at times, these efforts have been ineffectual. They have tried to achieve disclosure by enticing speakers (myself among them) to tell as many stories, theories, philosophies, reports, and conjectures as possible during these conferences. Sometimes these efforts have seemed to be such pointless exercises in gaining serious public attention that one might conclude they were intentionally designed to keep UFO phenomenon as the subject of ridicule. A cabal tactic used to maintain the secrecy would be to keep the public confused and unsure about the subject. At some of these UFO conferences, what is presented are unsupported statements and conjecture. This may be the main reason the mainstream media has not gotten on the bandwagon: there is little substance to talk about. The public is not clamoring for action because they simply don't know what or who to believe, so they take the path of least resistance: indifference. As long as the UFO phenomenon is defined by confusion and conjecture, there will be nothing specific to demand of our government. There is no hue and cry for a march on Washington demanding that disclosure happen now.

One of my principal objectives is certainly for disclosure of the truth of the UFO phenomenon. However, we find ourselves with the following "estimate of the situation." First, those who would keep disclosure from happening have done a masterful job of keeping the public disinformed and confused on the subject. That effort has no doubt been aided by well-placed agents acting as interested parties but really promoting ineffectual activities or encouraging true advocates to bicker among themselves or act in disunity. In addition, government agencies like the USAF, that probably have a substantial amount of information, have publicly presented an intense indifference to the subject, furthering the perception that there is nothing to be investigated.

Second, whenever claims are made, or "witness" reports without credible substantiation are presented, damage is done to the credibility of the phenomenon as a whole. Promoting such "ufology" topics as "free energy," controversial "insider" witnesses, and underground alien bases, although possibly having some basis in fact, have only served to provide more grist for ridicule. There seems to have evolved a culture where certain individuals or groups compete to be identified with having insider information or some special contacts with the aliens themselves, or they are making a living telling good stories at UFO conferences. That culture can only be detrimental to the objective of true disclosure.

Although the stated objectives of such groups profess the need for government disclosure, the result has appeared to be an eagerness to relate and support every wide-eyed story or speculation about the ET presence that anyone might come up with. There have been many other examples of individuals who are simply trying to promote their own notoriety. The public study of this phenomenon has evolved into another kind of game—the ufology game. What is the purpose of this game? Is it to get as many people to play as you can? Do we simply want a meandering mix of fact and fiction out there to titillate curiosity?

It is time we worked smarter toward the disclosure objective. We need to stop entertaining the public and simply inform the public as to the valid history of the phenomenon and the facts of particular cases. By "we," I mean each of us who has something to contribute or has an audience to speak to about the subject. We simply need to be responsible. We need to state clearly when we are relating substantiated fact and when we are simply speculating. If we want scientists to take a serious interest, we have to present our cases as scientifically as we can. I have always been open to any critique of my own case and to answering any question about what I present. My incident has been supported and substantiated by multiple witnesses and documentation. There are many other such valid cases. These are the ones that should be the center of exposure in trying to focus media and public attention on the phenomenon.

There are many conscientious researchers out there who have worked hard to validate incidents. There is much to present to a new congressional hearing by witnesses, and documents that could provide compelling evidence of the truth of the phenomenon. Let us focus on that, and decry those who would keep the phenomenon the subject of ridicule. I believe that the accumulation of the number of credible cases will eventually result in an overwhelming public outcry for disclosure. At that point, the zero-sum game will be over and governments will need to be accountable for this secret.

ADDENDUM—OCTOBER 2022

As of the time of this writing, the US Air Force (USAF) has not publicly commented on the Malmstrom AFB UFO incidents. I and other witnesses have spoken about them at press conferences in Washington, DC, at least four times. I have spoken openly during a span of twenty-six years at conferences in the US and fifteen other countries. This long silence from the USAF speaks volumes and is indicative of the extent of the institutionalized secrecy of UAP within other agencies of the US government (USGOV).

In late 2020, the Intelligence Authorization Act (IAA) was passed with a provision that required the director of National Intelligence to submit an intelligence assessment of the threat posed by unidentified aerial phenomena. National Intelligence issued its report, identified as a "preliminary assessment," on June 25, 2021, with input from over seventeen agencies. The report was a very limited evaluation of events that occurred between 2004 and 2021. The revelations and admissions stated in the unclassified executive summary included: "Most of the UAP reported probably do represent physical objects. . . . In a limited number of incidents, UAP reportedly appeared to exhibit unusual flight characteristics. . . . UAP clearly pose a safety of flight issue and may pose a challenge to US national security" (ODNI 2021, 3)

On October 19, 2021, I and other witnesses held a press conference and presentation at the National Press Club in Washington, DC, on the decades of UFO incidents at nuclear weapons facilities since 1944. It may have helped to spur further legislation. In November 2021, an amendment to the 2020 IAA was initiated by Sen. Gillibrand (NY). It included some extensive and detailed requirements for DOD/Intelligence Community (IC) involvement in the data accumulation, analysis, and reporting of the UAP. These include the requirement to investigate incidents at and around nuclear weapons facilities. Additional governmental action includes methods for allowing witnesses, who are currently under restrictions from speaking, to come forward with their testimony.

The 2023 amendment to the IAA includes requirements to investigate "trans-medium" objects. Those are objects that have been observed moving through airspace *and* bodies of water. Each of these recent legislative actions by the USGOV are a very welcome change to the decades of coverup and obfuscation by various agencies. They clearly indicate that the Congress, at least, has taken a strong interest in learning more about the UAP and prior involvement by various agencies.

The extreme secrecy with respect to UAP is likely to continue, albeit in a more subtle manner. The IC has had extensive experience in dealing with congressional committees with respect to matters of secrecy. Whatever information agencies are holding on UAP, it is likely as a result of activities in programs that are designated as SAPs, Unacknowledged SAPs, and CAPs. From decades of reporting on these programs to Congress, the IC, if they choose to do so, is capable of misdirection, obfuscation, and hiding what is really going on in those programs. This constitutes major obstacles in the process of achieving disclosure.

The problems of excessive secrecy are deeply entrenched within the USGOV. These have created a kind of internal corruption of the facts. Decisions that have been made about operational procedures (means and methods) in the past would be an integral part of how agencies and agents operate now. For example, the agencies involved in the UAP secrecy may have decided extraterrestrial technology might represent a threat to our national security. They may have also decided that UAP constitute an enemy of the US that must be defeated. In addition, new regulations may have been instituted in the interest of maintaining secrecy of UAP. These kinds of far-reaching decisions should require an announcement to, if not the acquiescence of, the public.

Another major factor for keeping the secrets may well be that the reputations of individuals in key positions could be compromised. That is, they would be asked to explain why particular secrets have been withheld from the public for such an extended period of time. They would have to give an account as to the question of whether or not secrets were held to benefit themselves or in the interest of the country. The challenge here is twofold: the perception of wrong-doing and/or corrupt intent.

As a result, we need to ask: What standards for ethical behavior should we rightly expect from a government official? Is lying to the public and to other agencies acceptable to maintain secrecy? How subjective is the level of importance ascribed to certain information? What rationalization has been done over decades to justify such excessive secrecy?

CHAPTER 4

The UFO Cabal

"Cabal: A conspiratorial group of plotters or intriguers."
— *THE AMERICAN HERITAGE DICTIONARY*

Yes, I am referring to a group involved in an international conspiracy of secrecy that is in control of the known facts of the UFO phenomenon. This is not a conspiracy theory; it is a conspiracy in reality. Two questions that may come to mind are: Why would there be such an organization? How could such an organization exist and survive without being discovered?

Human history is replete with accounts of secret societies. Some of these groups had, as their motive for being, objectives of doing some good for society. Others, such as the Black Hand, used violence and criminal activity for the purpose of achieving ill-gotten wealth. There are many models for secret societies, established for a multitude of different purposes.

FOLLOWING THE TRACKS OF THE UFO CABAL

Evidence points to the origins of the UFO cabal beginning as a result of the Roswell incident. The truth of the incident was initially told when the Air Force issued a press release stating that a saucer-shaped craft had been recovered near Roswell Army Air Field. The coverup of this most notorious of UFO incidents was ordered by the highest levels of government, most likely suggested by our military leaders at that time.

Soon after the initial press release, a false story of the recovery of a weather balloon was released on July 8, 1947, by General Roger Ramey, commander of the Eighth Air Force. The elements of the intelligence functions necessary for the implementation of a secrecy and suppression were implemented. The remains of the crashed craft and its occupants were collected and transported with a high level of secrecy by specialists in clandestine operations (Carey and Schmitt 2009). All known witnesses to this event, civilian and military, were contacted and forcefully directed to keep quiet about what they knew. Some were threatened with their lives and the lives of their loved ones if they did not maintain their silence.

When the Air Force declared the crash debris was simply a mistaken identification of a "weather balloon," they were setting themselves up as the purveyors of the truth of the matter, and if any of the witnesses disagreed, they would be going against the reputation and influence of a United States military power that had just won World War II and guaranteed our freedom and democratic way of life. This construct would have a major influence on the inception of the cabal. The "secret group" could be easily established because of the high political priority of maintaining our national security in the face of any and all enemies at this critical time when the Cold War was beginning and our military strength was paramount.

The Air Force program to study the UFO question started with Project Sign, which began in 1948. It was later called Project Grudge (an interesting choice of name). In March 1952, it was renamed Project Blue Book. Here is the Air Force explanation of this project:

> *The objectives of Project Blue Book are two-fold: First, to determine whether UFOs pose a threat to the security of the United States; and second, to determine whether any unique scientific information or advanced technology which could contribute to scientific or technical research. In the course of accomplishing these objectives, Project Blue Book strives to identify and explain all UFO sightings to the Air Force. (Feschino 2007, 2)*

The last sentence was not exactly true, as Captain Edward Ruppelt, the titular head of Blue Book, discovered he was not receiving all the details of reports of UFO encounters; some were classified as Secret, or above, and were not handled by his office.

On November 21, 1950, engineer Wilbert Smith wrote a memo to his employer, the Department of Transport of Canada, about his efforts to uncover information about investigations which were being carried on in relation to flying saucers (Birnes 2004, 291). He was of the opinion that his work on geomagnetics could be a link to "saucer" technology. He further wrote:

> *I made discreet inquiries through the Canadian embassy staff in Washington who were able to obtain for me the following information: a) The matter is the most highly classified subject in the United States Government, rating*

higher even than the H-bomb; b) Flying saucers exist; c) Their modus operandi is unknown but concentrated effort is being made by a small group headed by Dr. Vannevar Bush; d) The entire matter is considered by the United States authorities to be of tremendous significance. . . . I was further informed that the United States authorities are investigating along quite a number of lines which might possibly be related to the saucer such as mental phenomena. (Birnes 2004, 290–291)

This memo also indicates that the US Defense Research Board would be amenable to conducting some joint research with Canada on geomagnetics (Birnes 2004, 291).

There are some significant points to take from this memo related to the existence of a cabal. First, this secret group to study the UFO phenomena was well established by 1950 and headed by Dr. Vannevar Bush, who had been the most highly respected government advisor on science to the president during World War II. Second, this group was studying many different aspects of the phenomenon, which begs the question: How do you do scientific research without scientific facts? Vannevar Bush was a scientist, first and foremost; he would very likely have had access to recovered UFO/ET artifacts. Third, the United States was cooperating with other countries to work on these problems.

On July 1, 1952, a UFO was sighted over Washington, DC. One witness to this sighting was a George Washington University physics professor. He watched it for eight minutes, and he said it descended lower than the height of buildings in the city. The summer of '52 brought a wave of UFO sightings over Washington, DC. That summer there were 1,500 UFO sightings reported to Blue Book; 303 were unexplained. The summer of 1952 had more reported UFO sightings than any other three-month period in Blue Book's seventeen-year history. On July 28, 1952, the Office of Information for the Air Force stated, "The jet pilots are, and have been under orders to investigate unidentified objects and to shoot them down if they can't talk them down" (Feschino 2007, 3).

Harry Barnes was a principal Civil Aviation Administration (CAA, the precursor to the FAA) air traffic controller at National Airport who saw many of the UFO sightings in the summer of 1952 on his radar. He was given permission by the Air Force to give pilots headings to the unknowns that he saw on his radarscope. "Two or three times saucers darted away the instant he [Barnes] gave pilots directions for interception. . . . Barnes had an eerie feeling that the mysterious visitors were listening to his radio calls" (Feschino 2007, 33). During one intercept, a pilot heard his first name called out by a strange voice transmission. Military radio transmissions between aircraft do not use the first names of the pilots! No one was able to determine who or what made those transmissions. It appears that ETs understand our language and can mimic our voices! Later, Harry Barnes gave the following statement to the press: "There is no other conclusion I can reach but that for six hours on the morning of the 20th of July there were at least 10 unidentifiable objects moving above Washington. They were not ordinary aircraft" (34).

Notwithstanding the statements of Harry Barnes, the Air Force had two generals speak to the press about the

Washington sightings on July 29, 1952. Major General Roger Ramey, the same officer who had managed the debunking of the Roswell crash in 1947, and Brigadier General John Samford, director of Air Force Intelligence, would tell their audience that there are many forms of natural phenomena that could have caused people to see what wasn't really there. General Samford stated that most likely people were seeing the result of the reflection of ground images due to temperature "inversions." Later, two Harvard professors would publicly state their agreement with these conclusions. The campaign of disinformation, which Ramey had proven to be effective in blunting the interest in the Roswell case, would continue. However, the UFO sightings would also continue (Feschino 2007).

In January 1953, the Robertson Panel, a secret review of the UFO question by selected scientists, was convened and run by the CIA. In 1994, thanks to the efforts of research organizations such as Computer UFO Network (CUFON), the CIA released the Durant Report, a record of the panel meetings. The result was predictable: "After review and discussion of these cases (and about 15 others, in less detail), the panel concluded that reasonable explanations could be suggested for most sightings and by deduction and scientific method it could be induced (given additional data) that other cases might be explained in a similar manner" (Durant 1953, 7). In addition, the recommendations of the panel included: "The panel's concept of a broad educational program integrating efforts of all concerned agencies was that it should have two major aims: training and 'debunking'" (19). The "debunking" aim would result in a reduction of public interest in "flying saucers," which today evokes a strong psychological reaction. This education could be accomplished by mass media such as television, motion pictures, and popular articles.

Also included in the Durant Report was this:

> *The panel took cognizance of the existence of such groups as the "Civilian Flying Saucer Investigators" (Los Angeles) and the "Aerial Phenomena Research Organization" (Wisconsin). It was believed that such organizations should be watched because of their potentially great influence on mass thinking if widespread sightings should occur. The apparent irresponsibility and the possible use of such groups for subversive purposes should be kept in mind. (Durant 1953, 23–24)*

In these statements, the "secret group" would set its course for their activities in debunking UFO incidents and infiltrating UFO groups. It is very likely that public UFO groups have been and continue to be infiltrated by "moles" from intelligence agencies.

In 1962, there was another wave of sightings, and there was public demand for a congressional hearing. These hearings never took place due to the reversal of course by the very influential Admiral Roscoe Hillenkoetter:

> *Hillenkoetter was an extremely influential member of NICAP's board of directors. He had been the first director of the CIA from 1947–1950 . . . after his retirement he had made a statement to the press stressing the necessity of treating the UFO question openly and seriously. . . . "The Air Force has constantly misled the American public about UFOs. I urge congressional action to reduce the danger from secrecy." In 1962, however, as Congress was on the verge of open UFO hearings, Hillenkoetter abruptly resigned from the board and publicly stated that the Air Force UFO investigation should*

> *not be criticized anymore; the proposed 1962 hearings came*
> *to a crashing halt. (Druffel 2003, 89)*

In September 1964, Air Force Lieutenant Robert Jacobs videotaped UFOs circling the warhead section that had separated from an Atlas D missile during a test flight from Vandenberg Air Force Base. His supervisor, Major Florenze Mansmann, stated that after this video was shown to a group of high-ranking officers and agents of the CIA, the film and all copies were confiscated. Both of these witnesses have publicly verified these facts (Hastings 2008, 191–192). This is further testimony that the CIA was still involved in the coverup.

A similar incident had been reported on June 10, 1949, from the White Sands Missile Test Range. "When the missile had attained a speed of 2,000 feet per second on its upward flight, it was suddenly joined by two small circular objects that paced it, one on each side. One of the objects then passed through the missile's exhaust, joined the other, and together they accelerate upwards leaving the missile behind" (Hall 1988, 174–175).

The 1967 UFO incidents involving nuclear weapons bases (Malmstrom, Minot, and others) further intensified the effort toward secrecy of the phenomenon. There was an intentional, aggressive campaign by the Air Force to cover up these incidents and deny access to information about them.

From October 1969 to the present day, there has been an ongoing public policy of noninvolvement by the USAF in UFO investigations. This "official" USAF position is certainly not the truth of the matter. There have been a substantial number of incidents that have been investigated by the Air Force since 1969. (Some of these incidents will be covered in a later chapter.)

CABAL BASELINE ORGANIZATION

In the present day, we all recognize that governments worldwide have their secrets and the secret societies to control those secrets. As previously stated, under the umbrella of the US government alone, there are at least seventeen major intelligence agencies under the director for national intelligence. In addition to the specific intelligence tasks by these myriad agencies, the President's Office of Science and Technology proposed in its fiscal year 2013 budget to oversee $140 billion in research and development, the great majority of which was for expenditures of a classified nature.

In attempting to add scope to the operations of the cabal, we can start with the basic tenets of foreign intelligence. It can be defined as the "product resulting from the collection, processing, integration, evaluation, analysis, and interpretation of available information concerning foreign [entities]" (Richelson 2016, 1).

Following is what I consider to be the basis for a UFO cabal organization.

MAJOR ELEMENTS

Command and Control (CORE)

As indicated, there is no doubt that a select group composed of both government and civilians was initially formed to direct the study of the phenomenon. By the time it was established, this secret group would have as its primary charter: a) absolute secrecy from public disclosure; b) discovery and analysis of any and all aspects of the phenomenon; and c) evaluation and taking appropriate actions relative to our national security interests. There is little doubt that this program would have been given the highest security rating and priority. This CORE group:

- Directs all element functions.

- Is responsible to only itself for maintaining its charter objectives.

- Makes final decisions regarding ongoing operations.

Financial

Funding the various elements would be essential for such a large organization. In an organization such as this where success is paramount, there would be no question about acquiring the needed funds. Because this is a mixed government and civilian organization, funding would come from both of those sources. The motivation to provide all needed funding is not lacking from either sector. In the case of the US government, the potential benefit from UFO technology would be invaluable. In the case of civilian funding, the rewards from being on the ground floor of the information and knowledge gained from the phenomenon would also be invaluable. Funding through "black" projects is well hidden from scrutiny.

- US government black ops funds—requires direct Defense Department linkage at high level.

- Private international finance groups that interface at a very high level to CORE.
- Other agencies of the US government funding.

Facilities and Equipment

Facilities and equipment that could be used for storage, analysis, and research and development can easily be obtained through the use of existent or new facilities within the military-industrial complex. Industrial facilities are certainly available, considering the long-standing partnership between military and industry.

- Use agreements with secret Defense Department facilities—requires direct Defense Department linkage at high level.
- Interface with nonclassified civilian contracts.
- Interface with Defense Department supply and maintenance bases required.

ARTIFACT RETRIEVAL AND COLLECTION

This may be the largest element. It involves obtaining data and artifacts from many sources, foreign and domestic. Much of the data regarding civilian sightings and encounters is obtained from agents imbedded in public UFO organizations. There is ample evidence that intelligence agencies have been able to infiltrate these organizations and obtain information on the most significant sightings on a timely basis. On the recovery of artifacts (UFO craft) and actual bodies of ETs, there is also ample evidence that special groups, most likely military units, have been involved in retrieval operations. Army Sergeant Clifford Stone has written his account of being involved with a "recovery" team. He recalls one such recovery at Indian Town Gap, Pennsylvania, in 1969: "The craft was . . . I still refer to it as heel shaped . . . like the heel of a shoe. It had, like, a canopy, except the canopy didn't fly open like a canopy of a jet aircraft" (Stone 2011, 169).

The collection process requires isolation, protection, retrieval, operations secrecy, and storage. These require strong interface and coordination with other cabal elements.

- Products—UFO activity reports, evidence artifacts/samples, downed craft retrievals, information, and data.

- Interface and liaison with informants from civilian UFO groups, intelligence agents, military collection agencies (e.g., NORAD, NASA), monitoring stations.

- Direct interviews with witnesses.

Foreign Operations/Liaison

There seems to be little doubt that the US group, from the inception of the international cabal, has held a primary leadership role. As such, it likely has the principal role in the collection of foreign data and artifacts. In 2007, I was invited to speak in Ayacucho, Peru. While there, I made contact with an ex–Peruvian Air Force officer who informed me of a meeting he had attended with senior officers from his own country as well as the United States. He stated that during that meeting, the US officers told the Peruvian military present that they expected to receive information of UFO incidents of any significance. This is direct testimony of information flow to the US secret group.

After the Bentwaters Base incident in late 1980, a large team of US intelligence personnel descended on the base to interrogate, intimidate, and confuse witnesses in order to "control" the situation. It is very likely that these actions were done with the full knowledge and cooperation of the British authorities.

- Monitoring and coordination with foreign intelligence and military agencies.
- Contractual agreements may require State Department and Intelligence agencies' interface.
- Key function is collection.

Analyses

This is where the real UFO science happens. We probably have the most talented scientists and engineers in their fields looking carefully at the data and information gleaned from nearly seventy years of research on this subject. The problem is that much of cutting-edge science is being suppressed through classified research programs. And, as a result of this suppression, the new discoveries and concepts are kept from the public and our general scientific knowledge. This amounts to strict control of new knowledge by a small, select group. This situation is ripe for corruption and certainly counter to our demo-cratic form of government.

- Products—statistical techniques on collected infor-mation, employ scientists on various technological topics (propulsion systems, materials sciences, etc.), "think tank" reports related to deltas or changes to the ET presence.

- Paranormal attributes analyses. These are concepts such as invisibility, mind control, telepathic commu-nications, teleportation, etc.

- Key function: Writing reports for evaluation element.

Evaluation

In order to see where we humans stand with respect to the ET presence here on Earth, we need to evaluate their impact on all aspects of that presence. The prime concern is probably how our national security concerns are being affected. I suppose that the cabal has developed a good idea as to the objectives of ETs and is basing the ongoing evaluation on those objectives.

- Products—performs assessments based on analyses.

- Key function is to make "security risk" and major impact assessments from ET presence.

Security Operations

Security assurance throughout the entire organization is the prime directive for this element. One of the principal means by which a secret organization maintains its secrets is by assuming everyone else is a spy. Everyone in the organization is watched closely, no one is completely trusted, and detailed files are kept on everyone. There is currently a program within the Air Force, for example, that is called the "personnel reliability program." In this program, each person in some sensitive field is required to be evaluated with regard to their "reliability" in carrying out not just the letter of their responsibilities but the attitudes regarding the secrecy oath obligations. In the extreme, there would be new meaning to keeping a tight ship.

- Ensures secrecy at all operational levels through enforcement.

- Maintains a staff of security agents.

- Interfaces and liaises with Defense Department security agencies—requires interface at high level with the Defense Department.

Interpretation

This is the next step after review of the recommendations from the analysis function. The questions to be answered are: What is going on? How many incursions and where? Why are they doing what they are doing? How do we offset their actions? Can we do anything about it?

- This is a very high-level function because it entails decision-making at the highest levels. This is a CORE function.

- Key function is to issue directives to the lower echelons.

Integration

Whatever actions the CORE decides to take, they must be integrated across all elements.

- Directs element products to other elements.

- Ensures performance of the directives regarding those products.

- Evaluates outcomes of integrating those products.

- Sends reports and recommendations to CORE.

Industry Liaison

- Orchestrates technology transfer for commercial use.

- Oversees development of weaponry to counter perceived technological threat from ET technology.

- Develops planning for new/future industries related to ET technology.

Liaison—Extraterrestrial Intelligences

There have been a few publicly reported incidents that indicate that the cabal organization has indeed developed some sort of cooperative agreement with ETs. One example of this may be the Bentwaters case. In that case, there are multiple witnesses who claim high-ranking officers of Bentwaters Base anticipated contact with an ET craft. There have been other reports of meetings between government officials and ETs. As mentioned in the case involving Sergeant Stone, it is likely that specialized groups have been equipped and trained to interact and cooperate with the ET presence.

- This element requires very close interface with the CORE because of this highly sensitive, evolving relationship.

- Evaluation and analysis of the impact of this cooperation to US government and human considerations.

Compartmentalization is a key to keeping the secrets of the UFO cabal. "In any intelligence operation of a highly classified nature, the many segments involved are directed to operate only in their own little circle and not to enquire further without authorization and a 'need-to-know'" (Richelson 2016, 524).

Because "national security" would be a concern, there would be ongoing interpretation of the intent and objectives of ETs by the cabal. The sense of the security threat would be refined on an ongoing basis. It would certainly be interesting to learn how these concerns have changed over the years. I think there would have to be some prime motives within the core of such a complex organization in order for its continuation over the span of more than seventy years.

Raymond Fowler suggested in a letter to Roy Craig that the Secret Group would maintain the UFO secrets until four conditions existed:

1. Indisputable proof of their interplanetary nature,

2. Their purpose and motivation were known,

3. A control or means of defense by our country, and

4. A prepared public.

Fowler was trying to look at the possible rationale for public disclosure that could be used by a conscientious secret group. I think we must consider another strong impetus to maintain the secrets. The mere fact that this cabal has succeeded for more than seventy years in maintaining its secrets has made it a politically and financially powerful organization. In addition, it has the full support and backing of the US government, even though most in government are not even aware of its existence. And, even if there were a reasonable list of prerequisites necessary for disclosure, it would be up to the cabal to decide when those prerequisites were met.

Let us consider the kind of secrets that might be held by the cabal. Because it is reasonable to conclude they have had much greater access to these objects and beings, the cabal has very likely accumulated knowledge about some of what we would consider "fantastic" aspects of the phenomenon. We can certainly make an educated guess of what some of these may be, based on what has been observed and communicated to us. Here is a short list of those possibilities:

- ETs have a much longer life span than we have.

- They are able to transport themselves across enormous distances and at tremendous speeds.

- They may be mining precious commodities from other planets.

- They can make themselves and other objects invisible.

- They are able to transport themselves and others through seemingly impenetrable objects.

- They can easily overcome the forces of gravity and geomagnetics.

- They have amazing sources of power and can control natural energy sources.

If these possibilities are fact, then these secrets would be enormously valuable. Indeed, this may be the prime reason the cabal maintains its secrets—power and greed. The most corruptible commodities known to humankind!

ADDENDUM—OCTOBER 2022

I have written about my own experience while stationed at Wright-Patterson AFB in 1969. In that year, the USAF had decided at the public level not to further engage in the investigation or reporting of UFO incidents. Internally, they would continue their work on this phenomenon in a clandestine manner. As described previously, I am convinced there was an attempt to recruit me to join those secret operations in late 1969. All the meticulous secrecy surrounding the Malmstrom incidents is compelling evidence that there was and is a well-organized group of people within the USAF—operating within the larger group—that I refer to as the UFO cabal who are determined to ensure the secrecy of UAP.

If we consider this cabal as an organization that is highly capable of keeping its secrets, evaluate information, act on that information, recover craft, assimilate new technology, utilize that new technology, share information on a global scale, and effectuate some sort of defense against or cooperation with extraterrestrial beings, it must be one that is both complex and efficient.

The following accounts contribute to further justification for the existence of this cabal.

Based on documented witness testimony: On January 13, 1969, near the city of Varginha, Brazil, a crashed cylindrical UFO was investigated by the Brazilian army. There were at least two nonhuman entities that initially survived the crash, and debris was recovered, according to many witnesses. One week later, one of these nonhuman beings was seen in the city of Varginha, and three young ladies observed it at close range. It was described as having three clawed fingers and toes, oily brown skin, some nodules on its head, and large, protruding red eyes.

That being was captured shortly after this sighting. It had been badly injured and was taken to various hospitals for observation and treatment. However, it soon died in captivity. While it was at the hospital, US Embassy representatives were in attendance. After its death, an autopsy was performed by Dr. Badan Palhares. His driver has testified that Dr. Palhares spoke to his wife about that experience and informed her that the body of the being would be taken to the United States. If his testimony is true, it is indicative of many other instances where there has been close cooperation between the US and other nations on UAP.

The Bentwaters Base, near Rendlesham Forrest, UK, had a number of successive days of well-documented incidents, occurring in late December 1980. These are referred to as the "Rendlesham Forest incidents" (RFI). The RFI are also ones that demonstrate an organized response by members of multiple intelligence agencies from the US and UK, working jointly. Most of the witnesses to the events of sightings and landings of craft were interviewed by these agencies. Col. Charles Halt, a principal witness, has confirmed these interviews. During the interviews, many witnesses reported that drugs were administered to them. The specific drugs used have not been confirmed; however, it is known that a drug, such as sodium amytal, can be effective in allowing recall of memories in people who have experienced traumatic events. It can also be used to implant false memories. The details of the RFI by some witness testimonies have been inconsistent and contradictory. It is quite possible that these inconsistencies were a result of witness tampering, their testimonies having been induced while under the influence of drugs.

This is not the only case of drug-induced tampering with witness testimony by members of the intelligence community. The story of a 1976 UFO incident at Ellsworth AFB, South Dakota, as discussed in chapter 6, is another instance of drugs being used on witnesses. Lt. Col. Roger Doe (real name withheld on request) has testified to me that he was taken to a hospital after his incident, even though he was not ill nor complained of illness. He spent two weeks at the hospital. While there, he was interrogated by a member of the Office of Naval Intelligence (ONI). He states he was drugged during his interrogations. Why was ONI involved in an Air Force incident? Could it be that the US Navy is now the lead military agency on UAP?

Tactics that have been used to institute and maintain secrecy by the UFO cabal include ridicule and witness control. Ridicule of the subject has long been used so that witnesses and the public are discouraged from taking an incident seriously. After an incident, witnesses are sometimes dispersed through reassignment to stop any internal discussion of incidents. An example of this is the Malmstrom incidents. Many of those witnesses were transferred to other locations or positions after the incidents. Witnesses are also controlled through the USAF-instituted Personnel Reliability Program (PRP). On their performance evaluations, airmen were rated on how well they "toed the line" on Air Force policies, including not reporting UFO sightings. This was a method used for airmen to self-impose censorship of UFO incidents to improve their chances of promotions. And, as reported by witnesses, drugs have been used during interrogations to confuse, question recall of details, and/or to suggest false memories.

CHAPTER 5

The UFO Phenomenon

"Some people claim that extraterrestrials have already visited the Earth in the form of UFOs. Scientists usually roll their eyes when they hear about UFOs and dismiss the possibility because the distances between stars are so vast. But regardless of scientists' reactions, persistent reports of UFOs have not diminished over the years."
—DR. MICHIO KAKU, *PHYSICS OF THE IMPOSSIBLE*

When we were very young, much seemed phenomenal to us. The rising of the sun, the flight of birds, clouds changing shapes; all are amazing things to see. As we grow older, our parents, grandparents, teachers, and strangers tell us more about the nature of these things, and we begin the process of making assumptions about what is real and what remains mysterious. Also, we begin to simplify our understanding of the natural world by rationalizing these observations as the "way things are."

For most of us, there are simply too many observable things that we cannot fully understand because we simply don't have the time or knowledge to delve deeply into the scientific explanations. It may be that it is for some of these things that we also begin to provide ourselves explanations that are not based upon scientific analysis but some "metaphysical" analysis. I mean metaphysical in the sense that we are basing an explanation on something (e.g., religious beliefs, intuition) that is not in the realm of "scientific" reality. However, we should also consider that scientific facts are not all "set in concrete." In fact, some scientific "facts" have turned out to be incorrect based on later research. Thus we are left to conclude that explanations of reality, and in particular scientific reality, are exercises in probability. That is to say, an honest assessment of an observation may well be defined as a likely or probable explanation.

When discussing UFOs, we are faced with the further dilemma that we are observing new and unique phenomena that have never been explained or authenticated by some "official" or scientific authority. For some well-documented UFO incidents, we have observations of the phenomena for which we can present possible explanations by our current scientific methodology and standards. Others simply cannot be explained definitively.

One could argue that since the time of the first observations of unexplained aerial phenomena, we have been trying to understand the science behind what we saw. Unfortunately, the science we know simply does not seem to have answers for what we have observed in the UFO phenomenon. Ball lightning, swamp gas, or the planet Venus do not explain our collective experiences. Certainly, by July 1947, when the first nonhuman bodies— recovered from the Corona, New Mexico, crash site—were seen by doctors at Roswell Army Air Field, they knew it was some organic biology that they did not understand.

And when engineers inspected the wreckage of that craft at Wright-Patterson Air Force Base and found no visible means of propulsion or control, they also knew they had something more to learn about the physics of flight.

From the aggregate of reliably reported incidents, I am convinced that our government and other governments have access to the physical evidence of extraterrestrial craft and beings. I have no doubt that many scientists worldwide have studied the physical evidence and developed hypotheses to try to explain this "new" science. Of course, these studies have been done in secret and their results hidden from the public. It is reasonable to assume that some of this newly discovered science and its technological applications have been integrated into some of our own technological advancements. We may, for example, indeed have some alien technology flying in our modern civilian and military aircraft.

Is it right that this new science should be understood by just a few or for just the applications decided upon by a few? It is very likely that those who are keeping the UFO secrets would claim that the public has no "right" to know such secrets because they bear directly on "national security." Yes, the public has that right in a democracy; it is our nation and our security that are at stake. Those are the basic competing arguments for and against the disclosure of this reality.

PHENOMENAL STUFF

One of the advantages we observers now have is that many more attributes of this phenomenon have been reported since the first "modern" observations in 1947. For the purpose of understanding the scope of this topic, I will list and briefly comment on some of the more prominent attributes. The data presented here are based on information I have received from a multitude of sources and collected over the span of twenty-nine years of my own study and evaluation of the phenomenon. I make no claim that it is completely accurate in every respect. However, it is the result of my own best estimate of how the phenomenon has been seen.

UFO Craft

The flying objects, or craft, have been observed in a multitude of different shapes and sizes. They have been seen as small balls of light only a few inches in diameter to huge craft nearly a mile in length. Some of these objects have been seen as being translucent in appearance; that is, observers could look through the craft at objects on the other side. Nearly all observers have seen these craft fly at extremely high speeds. Nearly all report little or no sound as they fly or hover. There are many reports of observers seeing the objects disappear from one position and then instantly reappear in another position. Their shapes include oval, pear-shaped, spherical, triangular, rhombic, and amorphous.

There are some reports that claim they change shape in mid-flight. Many report seeing "windows" on the craft. There are also reports of small "fins" and other protuberances on some craft. The colors of craft also vary and include white, orange, blue, red, yellow, silver, and black. Many observers report that these colors are somehow more brilliant than they have ever seen before but also state that the light does not hurt their eyes. There are many reports of small, multicolored lights moving in a circular pattern on the lower surface of the craft. There have also been many reports of these craft shining a beam of light to the surface of the Earth. When landings have been observed, doors are seen on the craft.

There have also been a significant number of reports of radiation effects from these craft. Measurements of increases in radioactivity were made as early as 1950 at the Mt. Palomar Observatory in California after a "flyover" of a group of UFOs. Increased radioactivity was also detected as a result of the Bentwaters incident (1980) and the Lonnie Zamora sighting in Arizona (1964).

Extraterrestrial Entities

From reports of interactions with ETs by abductees and other observations, ETs are described in a variety of ways. In the case of the abduction of Travis Walton (1976), for example, he claims to have seen at least two kinds of ET. One was the typical "gray," small in stature with a large head and large black eyes. The other type he observed had fair skin and more human-like features. Some witnesses report seeing tall, insect-like creatures, and some report creatures with reptilian features. There are many variations in the appearance of these entities. Of course, we must consider the possibility that some of these apparent traits have been conceived from the imagination of the witnesses, or possibly reflect the intentional masking of their true nature by the ETs themselves.

These are some of the phenomenal aspects of these creatures that have been reported: They have been seen floating or defying gravity, and they seem to have the ability to pass through solid objects such as walls and windows. They seem to have powerful psychic abilities, including the ability to read our minds, possibly having some control over our thoughts or obscuring our memories. There are also reports of ETs having "healing" abilities.

Some interesting questions arise from this apparent zoology of ET races. Which are the more intelligent? Indeed, how would we presume to differentiate "intelligence" in them? Do they have conflicting objectives? Is one "superior" to another? What is their social structure like? There are innumerable questions about ETs.

The Abduction Phenomenon

Human abductions by ETs are a very real and pervasive aspect of the UFO phenomenon. There are some estimates by therapists and researchers that upward of a million people have been taken by ETs. Abductees are subjected to examinations and other "medical" procedures against their will. Many abductees have reported having objects implanted in their body. It is apparent that ETs have some objectives for this forced interaction with humans. Many abductees have reported that their reproductive organs have been tampered with, semen or ovum taken, and hybrid children produced. Others report they have been given messages regarding future events on Earth. There have also been a substantial number of reports of human children being taught some paranormal abilities, such as telekinesis.

This aspect of the UFO phenomenon seems to be the most frightening for most people. Of course, no one wants to be forcibly removed from their home in the middle of the night by nonhuman creatures. That is the stuff of horror movies and nightmares. However, because there have been so many reports by witnesses of such abductions, we must conclude these are very real and a worldwide phenomenon. The best explanation of the abduction phenomenon comes from people such as the late Dr. John Mack (1995, 96–110), a Harvard University psychiatrist who helped and counseled hundreds of abductees. The following is paraphrased from Dr. Mack's statements during an appearance on a television broadcast interview with Oprah Winfrey:

> When I first heard about this, I thought they were mentally disturbed. However, every case I have evaluated has stood on its own merit. This is not a club anyone wants to belong to. Hundreds of thousands, maybe millions of people have had very similar experiences. This is happening with children as young as two or three years old, so that rules out personality disorders. Many of these abductions are associated with physical findings. These people don't want to tell these stories. Most are terribly frightened and embarrassed by the telling of their experiences. These are people that make up every kind of person you can think of. The only thing that occurs like that is a real experience. If these experiences are real, what is going on?

> What typically happens is that a person is in their bedroom; a powerful blue light of energy comes on in the room. They see beings, and are taken or transported to a craft. The interior of the craft is a cool environment. They are put on a table and examined under a bright light. They undergo a traumatic experience of probing and examination. Sometimes

there are implants placed in their bodies, and sperm samples or women's eggs are taken. There is a whole pattern that after a while begins to become clear. We don't get very far trying to guess alien psychology. After the trauma of their experience, these beings want to make some sort of connection. They want abductees to look into their large eyes and have a deeper sense of connection with us. They don't understand why we are so aggressive. (OWN 1994)

I have spoken with people who have experienced the kind of abduction described by Dr. Mack (1995, 96–110). In fact, two of these experiencers have described being taken as young children. They both speak of being led to a kind of school setting with other abducted children. There, they are given something that looks like a "ball" or sphere to play with, and instructed to try to move the ball with their mind. It was as if the ETs were trying to teach some psychic skills to the children. I believe these people are telling the truth. Therefore, this brief description of their experiences provides us with more insight into the purpose for these abductions. (A more personal look at the abduction phenomenon will be presented in chapter 8.)

From this quick look at some of the remarkable aspects of this phenomenon, we can clearly see the kind of information that a secret cabal might have and its potential use and misuse. It is also apparent that, if access to artifacts and ETs were obtained, much of it could be "weaponized." It is irrational to think the military-industrial complex would walk away from such a potential "mother lode" of information, as is currently claimed by government agencies. The key to mining this valuable information is to keep the location of the "gold mine" secret from anyone else who might want the gold. Of course, the keepers of these secrets would argue that this information is a matter of "national security."

PROOF OF UFO PHENOMENA

The principal method by which government protects its secrets about the UFO phenomenon is by the simple claim that there is no "proof" of its existence. In November 2011, the Obama administration responded to numerous petitions for acknowledgment that there is an extraterrestrial presence on earth. The response from the Office of Science and Technology Policy was: "The U.S. government has no evidence that any life exists outside our planet, or that an extraterrestrial presence has contacted or engaged any member of the human race" (Atkinson 2011). There was no justification for this simplistic response. They did not cite any investigation or data used to come to this conclusion. The highest level of government simply dismissed the possibility and thereby dismissed the testimony of thousands of credible witnesses to the phenomenon, without giving it serious consideration.

In mathematics, there are specific methods for showing a "proof" of a postulate or theorem. The basic technique is to provide a mathematically valid rationale for each step in the process that demonstrates a proof. The reasons provided must be those that have been established as fact by mathematicians past and present through other "proofs." Because each statement in a proof is accepted as fact, it is a logical conclusion that the final statement or thesis of the theorem is also a fact, thus it has been proven.

Although mathematical proofs are intended to establish the validity of mathematical conjectures, the technique can certainly be applied to any question of the truth of a matter, including the question of the reality of the UFO phenomenon. After all, the primary utility of math is to apply it to real problems.

In 1948, after evaluating the quantity and quality of UFO reports that had come into the Air Force Project Sign database since mid-1947, the staff working on that project produced a report called "The Estimate of the Situation" for Air Force Chief of Staff Hoyt S. Vandenberg. The report included the evaluation of approximately six hundred sightings by military and civilian pilots and other witnesses. The report concluded that the UFO phenomenon was real and deserved to be taken seriously. Vandenberg disagreed and rejected the conclusions of the report. He stated there was no real proof of the phenomenon. Basically, he "pulled rank" and simply declared his conclusion without justification. (Generals don't have to justify their opinions to their subordinates.)

As a result, Project Sign was redesignated Project Grudge. According to Ruppelt, it was made clear to those on the project that the Air Force wanted to debunk the UFO phenomenon. Obviously a decision had been made at the highest levels that this phenomenon would be dealt with in two ways. Publicly, it would be "explained away" as a natural phenomenon. However, within the compact boundaries of a highly secret project, it would be investigated thoroughly.

The effort to disprove the existence of UFOs became a prime objective. Project Grudge was the more public face of Air Force interest in UFOs. It became a "zero-sum" game. Either the public believed UFOs were worth a serious look or it did not. It did not matter whether there was sufficient evidence to prove the existence of these objects; it was the public perception that mattered. In reality, Vandenberg must certainly have known about the recovered craft and bodies from Roswell. And he would have known there was absolute evidence that the craft and beings were from other worlds. However, he and the secret group had decided that, because they had the only "smoking gun" proof, and it was well hidden under cover of the highest secrecy, they could afford to claim there was no proof.

Thus, the real Air Force policy was born: Give a nod and a wink to the public whenever a sighting was reported, but explain away the majority of the sightings as natural events. This policy continued until 1969 when the Air Force manipulated the Condon Study to manufacture what it hoped would be a final estimate of the situation. The Air Force terminated Project Blue Book on December 17, 1969, basing its decision on the evaluation of the Condon Study (USAF Fact Sheet 2005). The current USAF policy became and still is "no comment" on the question of UFOs. In 2011, the office of the president of the United States blindly continued to support that policy.

Has the US government succeeded in disproving the phenomenon? No, obviously they have not proven that something does not exist, but they have worked hard to position themselves so that they don't have to respond to the question. By simply refusing to comment on the question in a meaningful way, the public/media perception is that it is not something that needs to be taken seriously. The media and the public have kowtowed on this question to the point at which questions are simply no longer asked. It is up to those of us who know better to continue to ask for answers. It is up to the community of serious researchers of this phenomenon to look at the evidence in a serious and scientific way. Therefore, there is no real attempt going on to prove the existence or nonexistence of the phenomenon.

THE SCIENCE OF UFOS

This puts those of us who are trying to evaluate the phenomenon in a rational manner at a distinct disadvantage. Scientists who might take an interest in this subject must consider the fact that they could lose government funding for their own programs if they did venture into serious consideration of UFOs. Such was the case with Dr. James McDonald.

McDonald was both a true scientist and a person with an abiding interest in the UFO phenomenon. That effort cost him dearly in his scientific career and in his personal life. During a congressional hearing in 1971 on the atmospheric effects of the supersonic transport aircraft (SST), McDonald testified as an expert in atmospheric research. One of the congressmen on the committee used McDonald's well-known interest in UFOs to embarrass and discredit him: Silvio Conte stated in the open hearing, "A man that comes here and tells me that the SST flying in the stratosphere is going to cause thousands of skin cancers has to back up his theory that there are little men flying around the sky" (Druffel 2003, 503).

Many serious researchers in this field find themselves scrambling for research funding. Though this makes the science of ufology more problematic, it does not mean that we cannot still pursue it. There have been some noteworthy attempts to do this kind of science.

Dr. Roger Leir has removed and analyzed artifacts from alleged abductees. His analyses have identified many anomalies. Some of these anomalies include: isotopic ratios of various element isotopes that vary significantly from those found on Earth; the presence of carbon nanotubes; the high level of magnetism; and the high incidence of nonmetallic inclusions in the metal. The analysis concludes that the artifacts are of manufactured, nonterrestrial origin (Leir 2005, 147–162).

Dr. Bruce Maccabee has performed an analysis of an acceleration of a UFO using video taken in 1995. His extensive and professional analysis calculated an acceleration of a startling 15,000 feet per second squared. That is equivalent to a g-force of 500 g (Maccabee 1996, 183–217)!

Lloyd Pye published a genetic study of a 900-year-old, nonhuman appearing skull discovered around 1930. A DNA analysis of this skull was done by geneticists Dr. Malhi and Dr. Eshleman. A small fragment of the nucleotide sequence of the skull's DNA showed an amazing seventeen differences to the comparable human DNA sequence (Pye 2010).

At the Roswell UFO festival in July 2012, Frank Kembler presented his evidence from a small artifact he had found at the debris site of the 1947 crash near Roswell. He also had his artifact analyzed by an accredited metallurgical laboratory. His artifact (AH-1) also showed a significant difference in isotopic ratios from that found on Earth.

There is also the work of Jean-Pierre Petit, who has published many scientific papers on magneto-hydrodynamics (MHD). His body of work, including experimental results, shows that it is possible to eliminate leading edge shock waves from craft flying at hypersonic speeds. By eliminating these shock waves, airborne craft are able to maneuver quietly at very high velocities. In fact, this technology has been applied to the newest of our aircraft such as the Aurora and Russian-made Ajax craft. This technology is similar to that which has been observed in UFOs (Petit, Geffray, and David 2009).

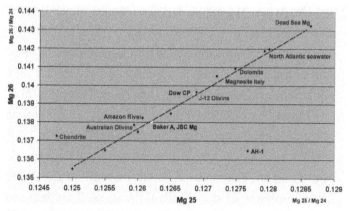

Magnesium isotopic ratio of Roswell artifact. Courtesy of Frank Kembler.

These are just some examples that could be presented to scientists anywhere in the world for their review in consideration of the extraterrestrial hypothesis. Some of these studies should be repeated to show consistency of the results. All that is needed to demonstrate scientifically that we are dealing with a real, observable phenomenon is a relatively small amount of funding. However, serious funding sources will not likely come forward unless and until the entire subject of UFOs is once again taken seriously.

We can all help. Even if we have only a passing interest in the subject of UFOs, we don't have to dumb down the scientific aspect of the phenomenon. Too many times, the phenomenal aspects of this subject are emphasized in a way to make them too otherworldly or inexplicable. To move forward, we must at least attempt to describe these amazing experiences so that we can demonstrate we are trying to take the scientific approach to explain them to the rest of the world.

CHAPTER 6

The Stories of Others

I have often been contacted by people who wanted to tell me their stories of encounters with UFOs. Of course, I am well aware that some people may wish to promote stories they know are false or that have been deliberately modified to make them sound more fantastic. I have had to rely on my own judgment when trying to evaluate the veracity of stories. Initially, I rejected even considering many of the stories I heard because they simply did not fit into what I considered rational. As time went on, I began to realize that none of these stories, true or otherwise, makes rational sense relative to what we think we know about the real world. The reality is that these objects and their occupants are phenomenal with respect to our reality.

In addition, I realized that our "science" is not static or inviolate. For example, in 2012 there was an announcement by the scientific community that there have been corroborating tests indicating that the speed of light is not the greatest possible speed that a quantum particle can obtain! However, more recently the accuracy of the tests by which this result was reached are being questioned. Although we do apply the science we know every day, clearly some scientific principles are subject to change as we continue to expand our knowledge.

My thinking about the UFO phenomenon has evolved to where I now don't immediately discount any story that I hear. I try to be more open to the possibility that some new story could have validity, and I take more time to consider it based on the totality of my own experience and research. Eventually, however, in order to continue to try to make some sense of the entire phenomenon in my own mind, I must either accept or reject the stories that I hear. Again, these judgments are simply my own, and I certainly do not claim they are the final word as to the stories' truthfulness.

To complicate matters, some deliberately false stories are promoted by the cabal in order to disinform the public and bring further ridicule or confusion to the subject of UFOs. As a result, I have changed my mind about a few cases. I think my opinion about these cases changed because I did not recognize the truly phenomenal nature of this subject. My thoughts about this phenomenon have evolved.

The stories of others that I present in this chapter are those that I consider as having a high level of credibility based on my own judgment. I make no claim or try to offer proof that they are absolutely true. However, based on what I have learned from my experiences and research over the years, I am convinced that they are, indeed, true accounts.

CAMP NEW AMSTERDAM, NETHERLANDS, 1979 — JOSIE ZWINENBERG

In 1979, the US Air Force had an operational unit based at what they called Camp New Amsterdam. It was located at Soesterberg Air Force Base in the Netherlands, near the town of Soesterberg. This unit, the 32nd Tactical Fighter Squadron, was assigned a tactical combat mission in support of NATO. In early 1979, the squadron began using the F-15 fighter aircraft. Some models of the F-15 were capable of carrying a tactical nuclear weapon (B-61). Nuclear weapons were stored on the base.

On the afternoon of February 2, 1979, Josie Zwinenberg was riding her horse along an area known as the Leusderheide, about five kilometers (about three miles) from the Soesterberg base. As she approached the highest point of this area, she brought her horse to a stop and looked out at a stand of trees about 750 meters (about a half mile) away. There, she saw an object silently hovering above the trees. She estimated the object was thirty to fifty meters (about 100 to 165 feet) in length. It was not an aircraft of any type she had ever seen. Living near Soesterberg, she had seen many different aircraft fly in and out of the base, but nothing like this object hovering above the trees.

This object had many bright white lights interspaced with blue lights. The lights were so bright that she could not make out the exact shape of the craft. She sat on her horse, in awe of what she was seeing. This object made no noise and seemed to be perfectly still. She was amazed by the color of the blue lights, saying it was the brightest blue she had ever seen. Though the lights were very bright, it did not hurt her eyes to look directly at them. She watched the object for a full fifteen minutes and noticed that it did not seem to be affected by gravity at all; it was perfectly motionless the entire time. She approached the object on horseback and kept it in view until she reached the trees. At that point, she stopped under the trees to try to look underneath the object. Then she was distracted by some rustling sounds coming from the brush in the forest. Her horse also reacted to the sounds. When she looked up again, the object was gone.

This sighting turned out to be a prelude to what would occur on the next day. On February 3, 1979, an object with three very bright white lights and one red light flew at an altitude of 150 to 200 meters (about 500 to 650 feet) and an average speed of fifty to one hundred kilometers per hour (about thirty to sixty miles per hour) over the flight line of the Soesterberg base. At times, it was seen to emit a beam of light to the ground. The object did not make a sound and was seen by many airmen at the base. The object twice flew along the flight line before departing at a high rate of speed. This was the summary of an investigative report by three members of the working group NOBOVO, including Dr. W. de Graaff, who worked at the Astronomical Institute (Griffioen 2018).

There is more to Josie's story. In the summer of 2011, while on vacation in Ireland, Josie Zwinenberg was approached by a man who called himself Tom. She had never met this man before, but he soon told her about the details of her encounter with the UFO some thirty-one years earlier. Included in those details was the fact that she heard sounds coming from the bushes during the encounter. This was a piece of information she had not told anyone, so there is no way anyone else could have known that unless they were there. He proceeded to tell her that "they" had been observing her since the incident in 1979.

I point this out to emphasize the fact that witnesses are tracked by the cabal for long periods of time. How can this be? Would intelligence agencies really spend the money and manpower to track certain witnesses to UFO events? As the record of treatment of witnesses to the Roswell incident indicates, they would do exactly that if they thought the occurrence had enough significance to be problematic to their objectives of hiding the facts from the public. The obfuscation of the facts of a significant incident may involve intimidation of witnesses through methods such as ridicule, or the threat of ridicule, up to and including harsher methods such as physical threats. It is a testament to her courage that Josie has chosen to come forward with her story.

BEALE AIR FORCE BASE, 1959 — JOHN MULLICAN

John Mullican was still a boy of sixteen in December 1958 when he moved from Indiana to Smartsville, California, a small town near Marysville. He and his younger sister helped their mother run the Beale Junction Restaurant and Service Station. It was not far from Beale Air Force Base. In early 1959, Beale was a part of the Strategic Air Command and had a B-52 bomber squadron located there. In 1961, it had one of the first Titan I intercontinental ballistic missile (ICBM) squadrons. Clearly, Beale was a nuclear weapons base during this period.

John recalls that it was right after the B-52s came to Beale that he began seeing UFOs in the night sky over the diner. They would appear in groups of three. Then it would not be long before he would hear Air Force inter-ceptors flying overhead to chase them. He recalls that the objects seemed to accelerate almost instantly. They could make ninety-degree turns. Of course, the Air Force jets were never able to catch them, and it seemed to John that the UFOs enjoyed the chase because that scenario occurred frequently.

One evening in 1959, there was a mass sighting of about fifteen UFOs overhead. John, his mother, and his sister all observed these objects. That night turned out to be a very unusual sighting. At first, the Air Force sent chase planes after them. Later that evening, after the planes had returned to Beale, the entire group of fifteen UFOs returned. One of the objects flew directly over the diner and hovered nearby. In a March 10, 2007, letter to me, John recalls:

> The saucer stops and instantly turns on the most beautifully colored lights I had ever seen. They were all around the sharp edge of the saucer . . . there was a dome on the top . . . with three windows in it. The top of the dome had a slight arch on its top . . . the windows were taller than they were wide . . . we were looking at three almost like people. Their heads were a little large with small bodies . . . all three of them waved at us. . . . I don't know what made me do it but I waved back at them, I had the most peaceful feeling come over me like maybe they were family.

John later described this feeling as euphoric. It triggered a deep realization that not only are we not alone but we are also part of a community of different life forms.

The evening was not over. John, his mother, and his sister then heard a humming sound like the loud buzz coming from an electrical transformer: "Then here comes this huge ball of a brilliant white light 'ship.' . . . I could hear a slight purr like from an engine as it passed in front of us, but no sound as it went past us. The 'space ship' was twice the size or bigger than a house. . . . I could see a white-like gas form around it and a long tapered vapor coming off it into a tail. The gases totally engulfed it."

Relative to what John described, I had years earlier received a copy of an Air Force telex, shown here. This telex was sent from a radar station near Kalispell, Montana, in September 1967. It is an official UFO report that speaks to the kind of "white haze" seen by John.

```
   PTTENK686PTTUZYUW RUWTENBO767 2592349-UUUU--RUWNFVA RUEDFIF RUEDHQA.
ZNR UUUUU                             1967 SEP 17  00 25
P 162210Z SEP 67
FM 716 RADAR SQ KALISPELL AFS MONT
TO RUWNFVA/ADC ENT AFB COLO
RUWTENB/28 ADIV WALMSTROM AFB MONT
RUEDFIF/FTD WPAFB OHIO
RUEDHQA/CSAF WASHINGTON DC
RUEDHQA/OSAF WASHINGTON DC
BT
UNCLAS 716OPS 00324 16 SEP 67. FOR AFRDC, FOR TDETR, FOR
SAF-OI. U.F.O REPORT 16 SEP 67.
NAME: MR A. Z. LIEWIS
TIME: 14440Z
PLACE: COLUMBIA FALLS, MONT
ONE OBJECT FLYING ABOUT 40,000 FT., EAST TO WEST DIRECTION TOWARDS
WHITEFISH, MONT. OBJECT WAS LAST SEEN GOING DOWN EAST OF THE
MOUNTAINS FOR TO FIVE MILES OF WHITEFISH, MONT. THIS OBJECT
WAS SEEN FLASHING A LIGHT OFF AND ON, AND A WHITE HAZE LIKE SMOKE
WAS UNDER THE OBJECT.
TELEPHONE: 892-4103
OBJECT WAS SEEN FOR FOUR MINUTES.
BT

NNNN
```

Telex describing 1967 UFO sighting

John also had a more personal experience with these entities. One evening he awoke to the sight of a beautiful girl standing next to his bed. He couldn't believe his eyes. He remembers that her eyes were "bluer than the sky." Standing next to the girl was a childlike "gray" type and also a taller "gray." He recalls the feeling that they were thanking him. They then proceeded to "float" to their UFO craft, which was just sitting on the ground outside the trailer where he lived. Later, John felt a lot of pain in his groin area. The pain stayed with him for two days.

John sent me a photograph of one object that was taken with a 35 mm Kodak Instamatic. It shows the smoke ring that was left after the UFO departed at high speed during one of his sightings.

Compare John's photo below to one of the photos taken by Rex Heflin (facing) in 1965. In each case, photos were taken as the craft departed at high speed. An analysis of this Heflin photo postulated that the UFO had acquired a coating of soot from the notorious LA smog and somehow discharged that soot as it departed.

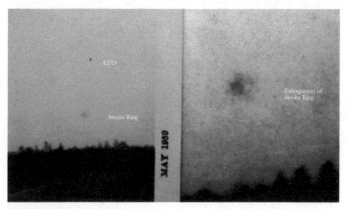

John's photo

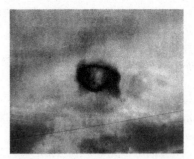

Rex's photo of UFOs leaving smoke rings.

An article in *Science* magazine warned that a study found that soot is warming the climate about twice as fast as scientists had estimated. Eight million tons of soot are produced each year by burning fossil fuels (Kerr 2013, 382).

CAMP SLAYER, IRAQ, 2006— MARK KOCH

On August 13, 2006, Sergeant First Class (SFC) Mark Koch was the first sergeant with a platoon of twenty-five men at the Radwahnian Palace complex, located southwest of Camp Slayer. At approximately ten p.m., they were on a routine patrol though the town of Makasib and traveling north toward Baghdad International Airport. It is important to note that Mark and his platoon routinely took this route through the town of Makasib and had done so the previous day. On this night, his gunner radioed to stop the patrol. Mark told me in a 2006 interview:

> *We performed a security halt and dismounted the vehicles. This was normal procedure when someone spotted a situation that could be a danger to the platoon. The gunner said,*

"It's not on the ground, it's up here. Look up!" I looked up and what I thought I saw it was something manufactured. It looked like landing lights propped on thousand-foot-tall poles. We looked at it for three to five minutes. All twenty-five of us looked up! Then we put on our night-vision goggles. It looked solid. You could not see the stars between the lights. It was triangular with each side of the triangle equal in length. It had lights on only the leading edge, in the shape of a "V." The lights were colored white-orange. There were about four to five lights on each side. The brightness of the lights looked muted; sort of milky white. One of the other men said, with the goggles on you could see the reflection of the city lights underneath. I saw a smooth surface. There were no rivets, no seams, no exhaust ports, and no sound. It was, totally, silent. I did not think it was moving, but some of the other men said it was moving slowly. Each side was about four football fields [1,200 feet] in length. It was enormous. It basically covered the entire town of Makasib!

The image shown here is a depiction of the object described by SFC Koch. The runway lights of Baghdad International Airport are visible to the North.

Artist's depiction of craft

Mark continues:

My first thought was that this was some kind of observation platform the army had built. I thought that this platform had to be supported by poles. I thought to myself, "How did they get those poles up so fast?" We had been through here the previous night. But then I looked closer and realized there were no poles. After about five to seven minutes, I decided we have to move to meet our next scheduled checkpoint. We went really fast through Makasib to get to the other side. It took us about five minutes. We were all anxious to get another look at this object from a distance. When we got to the fruit tree groves, we looked back and it was gone. I told the lieutenant I thought it would have been a mistake to report what we had seen. I told him that if we did report it, we would be laughed at and probably lose our rank and chance of promotion. He agreed.

When we got to headquarters, I simply asked if anything was going on. They said no. However, they did not have direct communication with the Air Traffic Control tower. So, it is possible that people in the tower did see or have a record of the appearance of the object. Later, I met separately with the men in my platoon and told them that yes, we saw something bizarre, but I would not spread the story too much unless you want to get laughed at. Most of them agreed to keep it to themselves. However, since my separation from the service, I have talked to all the staff sergeants and four or five E-5s and six or seven privates and specialists at company reunions. They have not forgotten what they saw and there remains a lot of interest in talking about it.

This is the first time SFC Koch has discussed his story openly. He has contacted some of the other witnesses to this incident, although many of them are still on active duty. He anticipates that some of them will want to come forward also with more details. I, too, anticipate that more witnesses and details will come forth. Until then, this story is to be continued.

WHITEMAN AIR FORCE BASE, MISSOURI, 1976 — JANE DOE

Jane (not her real name) was newly married in the fall of 1976. Her husband (name withheld on request) was an Air Force security guard at the Whiteman missile sites. She recalls local news reports of UFO sightings and cattle mutilations. Jane worked as a nurse at an off-base hospital.

On one particular night in the fall of 1976, she was dropping off a fellow nurse on base. She recalls entering the base through the Knob Noster gate. As they came up to the gate, she was wondering why the security policeman (SP) at the gate was not out front by the security shack. They stopped at the gate and waited for someone to approach them about entry to the base. After a few minutes, she tapped her horn and an SP approached them holding field glasses and waved them through. After she dropped her friend at her house on base, Jane traveled back to the same gate she had entered. She recounted in a September 2010 letter to me:

> *The closer I got to the flight line I noticed more and more military cars and jeeps on either side of the road. . . . I noticed an abnormally large number of lights focused on the flight line . . . a lot of people were heading to the end fence on the flight line . . . most were looking up. I leaned forward to look, too. To my shock, I saw a saucer shaped object hovering directly overhead. The area directly below it was Alpha silo. I was startled by an SP tapping on my hood as he waved me toward the exit.*

By the time she reached home she could still see the bright lights along the flight line. When her husband returned from his tour of duty at the site, he said, "Did you see the UFO? It came over all the missile sites. They changed all the launch codes!"

ELLSWORTH AIR FORCE BASE, SOUTH DAKOTA, 1976— LIEUTENANT COLONEL ROGER DOE

Roger (not his real name) was a newly appointed Missile Combat Crew commander in May 1975. He was assigned to the 44th Missile Wing, Ellsworth Air Force Base. Sometime on one evening in July 1976, he was on alert duty monitoring the ten Minuteman II missiles under his command when he received a call from his security guard upstairs.

"Sir, I have to report that we are under attack by a UFO," the guard said. Roger could also hear the sound of M-16 rounds being fired in the background. Without direction from him, the guards had started firing their weapons at the UFO as it hovered over the fenced area of the Launch Control Facility. Roger then watched the indicators on his status board alternately displaying "Ready to Launch" or "Missile Fault." He was kept busy for the next few minutes frantically trying to issue "Inhibit" commands to prevent any launch procedure sequence. After about five minutes, the guard called back and reported that the UFO had departed and the guards had expended all their ammunition!

After that call, Roger notes that something highly unusual happened. He waited a full ten minutes or more to report the incident to the command post. He had ten minutes of missing time that he cannot account for. His crew was relieved the next morning and they were flown back to the base. At the base headquarters he was interrogated/debriefed by an officer from the Office of Naval Intelligence (ONI), even though this was strictly an Air Force base and an Air Force Office of Special Investigations (AFOSI) was located on base.

Immediately after this interrogation, Roger was placed in an isolated ward of the base hospital for two weeks, even though he had not complained of nor knew of any medical problems that he had. After his release from the hospital, he was ordered to go back to his hometown to recover from some illness he did not have. He was actually given orders to take medical leave from duty and return to his hometown. He was driven to the airport directly from the hospital. He was ordered to remain at home for six weeks!

I was an active duty officer for seven years and had never heard of such a procedure. Roger recalls that while in the base hospital he was given many different types of drugs and subjected to hypnosis. He eventually returned to missile duty at Ellsworth but recalls that some sort of special black box was placed in his capsule that was supposedly used to monitor electrical activity there.

It is interesting to note that according to an article published in the *MUFON Journal* in July 2008, a very similar monitoring program had been conducted over a period of three years, ending in 2003. It was called the Ambient Monitoring Project (AMP). AMP was conducted by the UFO Research Coalition (URC), which included the Center for UFO Studies (CUFOS), the Fund for UFO Research (FUFOR), and Mutual UFO Network (MUFON). AMP involved placing a "black box" filled with various electromagnetic and other sensors that measured temperature, humidity, and barometric pressure in the homes of people who were alleged to have been repeat abduction experiencers. These boxes were placed in the bedrooms of these subjects. The purpose of the box was to detect and record various energy/temperature/auditory variations in the room during the evening. If the subjects suspected that they had been abducted, they were to send the recording from the box to a location where it would be analyzed. The objective of this experiment was to obtain some physical evidence that would indicate an ET visit had occurred. No definitive results of the AMP project have ever been published.

Was there a connection between these two "black box" programs—one conducted under classified conditions by intelligence agents and the other more openly? Of course the objective of each was the same—to collect evidence of abductions.

BENTWATERS BASE, UK, 1980

This incident was witnessed by many US Air Force officers and airmen who were stationed at this NATO base. It is important to note that Bentwaters was a nuclear weapons base. This incident has received a lot of attention because of the release of tape recording from one of the sightings by Lieutenant Colonel Charles Halt, deputy base commander at Bentwaters Base. It has also received a lot of attention because of the differences in the stories told by some of the witnesses.

I will not review this case in detail here because it has been reviewed and discussed in great detail in books like *Left at East Gate* (Warren and Robbins 1997) and others. The basic assertions in this case are that, over the span of three days in late December 1980, UFOs were seen in Rendlesham Forest, adjoining the base. One witness, James Penniston, claims to have approached and touched a landed craft and received some messages. Another witness, Larry Warren, claims to have seen strange beings emerge from a craft who may have communicated with high-ranking Air Force officers while many other airmen and even civilian personnel looked on.

The difficulty with believing the whole cloth of the Bentwaters case is that, in my opinion, some of the facts that were asserted have conflicted with statements of other witnesses. In addition, some of the witness statements have changed over the years. However, one aspect of the stories of the Bentwaters case is consistent: Many of the witnesses claim to having been interrogated at length by members of the military or civilian intelligence agents. Some witnesses claim to have been drugged and subjected to other extreme methods, such as sleep deprivation, during these interrogations.

This seems to correlate with Colonel Doe's statement with respect to the 1976 Ellsworth base incident. He, too, claimed that he was interrogated after being administered drugs. That would suggest an intentional attempt to confuse or alter the memories and testimonies of witnesses. The obvious purpose of these efforts would be to discredit the incident from within. This tactic seems to have worked, because the Bentwaters case remains, in my mind, an enigma of partial truths and conflicted facts.

MALMSTROM AIR FORCE BASE, MONTANA, 1967

On the afternoon of March 24, 1967, the same day as my own incident, Airman Sidney Young was driving southwest on Montana Highway 200, about twenty miles from Great Falls. In a personal communication to me in December 2012, he recalls:

> At approximately five to six miles southwest of G-7 (it is located near highway 200) is where I stopped to look, facing north towards Augusta. I would guesstimate its distance at six to eight miles away. Draw a circle that includes G-10 and F-07, and the object had to be within that circle. [Note: G-10 and F-07 are missile launch facilities.] After careful study of road maps and your launch site map I am positive as to viewing position.

As he crossed the Dearborn River, Airman Young was astonished to see a huge beam of light coming down from the sky. He estimated that the diameter of this beam was at least the length of a football field. He couldn't estimate the length because it came through some low clouds. He knew it was not a beam of sunlight because he could see the sun to the southwest. He says, "At the time that this occurred, the only thing my brain could compute was this thing must have been a gigantic ray of light."

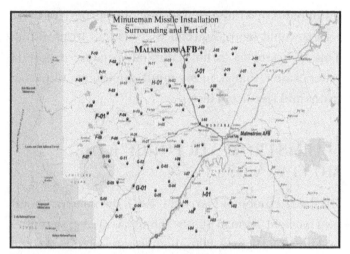

341 Strategic Missile Wing, Malmstrom AFB, Montana

However, after viewing a video of a large cylindrical-shaped UFO, he says, "I am convinced now this is what I was staring at for over five minutes. Thinking back now, it understandable why the edges of this cylinder shape were so sharply defined and more importantly there was absolutely no spill-out of light either up where it entered the cloud cover or down at the ground. This simply had to be a solid, white-colored cylinder shape standing there in a fixed position." The map pictured above shows the location of the Minuteman missile field west of Malmstrom. Again, it appears that ETs wanted to shine a light on our nuclear weapons; a very large light!

Later that same day, March 24, 1967, there would be other sightings of UFOs. At about seven p.m., while driving through the town of Belt, thirty miles to the east of Syd Young's sighting, truck driver Ken Williams observed a UFO at close range. The details of the Belt sighting were discussed previously.

This is not the only observation of a very long, very wide, cylindrical-shaped object. In October 2012, a similar cylindrical object of enormous size was video recorded entering the volcano Mt. Popocatepetl, Mexico. Because the camera used to record that video is operated by the Mexican government to record the activity of the volcano on a twenty-four-hour basis, it is clear evidence of this type and size of object.

CHAPTER 7

A Strange Love of Nukes

*"The catastrophe of the atomic bombs which shook men
out of cities and businesses and economic relations
shook them also out of their old established habits of
thought, and out of the lightly held beliefs and preju-
dices that came down to them from the past."*
      —H. G. WELLS, *THE WORLD SET FREE*
      ([1914] 2015, 106)

In 1967, my Air Force job was to sit in an underground
concrete capsule where my commander and I had control of ten Minuteman I missiles. Each missile had a single
nuclear warhead that had a capacity for destruction the
equivalent of nearly one million tons of TNT—enough to
engulf the center of any major city in a single ball of fire.

In that year, US military forces had a stockpile of
about 37,000 nuclear bombs. The USSR had stockpiled
about 45,000 nuclear bombs. Of course neither country
needed such large stockpiles of nuclear bombs, because
the 10,000 or so bombs that each was capable of launch-
ing against the other would be more than adequate for

the total destruction of human civilization and most other life forms on planet Earth. The year 1967 was the peak of our insane national security policy, appropriately called Mutually Assured Destruction (MAD). How did humanity manage to bring itself to that point?

THE START OF THE NUCLEAR AGE

By the beginning of the 20th century, the term "radioactivity," referring to the energetic emanations detected as radio waves coming from certain elements, was being used by science. Scientists like Marie and Pierre Curie and Ernest Rutherford had already discovered that certain radioactive elements such as thorium, actinium, and radium could disintegrate and produce other elements, or undergo a transmutation. Rutherford was later to accomplish an artificial disintegration of atoms of nitrogen resulting from the collision with alpha particles. In 1904, he published evidence that the heat produced by radioactivity was much greater than any chemical reaction. These and other scientific breakthroughs marked the beginning of the search for and application of nuclear energy.

In 1914, H. G. Wells wrote the fictional book *The World Set Free*. As with many of his works, Wells displayed some amazing insights in this book. He predicted the atom bomb would be developed in 1933 ("he set up atomic disintegration in a minute particle of bismuth, it exploded with great violence into a heavy gas of extreme radioactivity" [2015, 21]). Nuclear fission was, in fact, first demonstrated in 1938. Wells predicted the first nuclear power plant ("It was in 1953 that the first [atomic] engine brought induced radioactivity in the sphere of industrial production and its first general use was to replace the steam engine and electrical generating stations" [2015, 26]). In reality, it was 1954 when the USSR built the first nuclear power plant to generate electricity for a power grid. In what would later be an amazing sequence of events, these predictions and this book would eventually play a role in the US effort to build the first atomic bomb.

By early 1937, physicists Lise Meitner, Otto Hahn, and Fritz Strassmann of Germany had devised experiments to bombard a sample of uranium isotope with neutrons. In December 1938, although Meitner was in exile after the German Anschluss with Austria, that experiment succeeded. It succeeded in splitting the uranium atom, transmuting it to barium, and the release of energy. The energy release per atom was small, but relative to the size of the atom, it was enormous.

The news of the discovery of uranium fission was received by another émigré from Nazi Germany, Leo Szilard. In early 1939, Szilard was also a nuclear physicist who had known Lise Meitner and Otto Hahn. He later wrote: "When I heard this I immediately saw that these fragments, being heavier than corresponds to their charge, must emit neutrons, and if enough neutrons are emitted, then it should be, of course possible to sustain a chain reaction. All the things which H. G. Wells predicted appeared suddenly real to me" (Rhodes 1986, 266). Szilard was a great fan of H. G. Wells and he had never forgotten Wells's book *The World Set Free*.

Well before December 1942, when Enrico Fermi produced a chain reaction of nuclear fission from neutron bombardment, it was clear to many that this discovery could be used to develop a bomb that would release enormous amounts of energy. The military application suggested by these results became evident, but for reasons lost to history, the German military did not pursue the development of the bomb with any dedication or urgency. The United States, too, would not have pursued this weapon of unimaginable power had it not been for the efforts of Szilard and Albert Einstein.

In a letter to Franklin Roosevelt, the two highly respected scientists had proposed the critical necessity of developing this weapon before the Nazis and Adolf Hitler could acquire it. The program to study the possibility of an atomic bomb was initiated by FDR after the United States entered World War II in 1941. The program was known as the Uranium Committee. But it was not until February 1942 that bomb development was given the highest priority; by then it had become obvious that both the Germans and Japanese, intent on world domination, had also begun to study the feasibility of constructing an atomic bomb. The bomb was forced to become a reality out of the darkest fears of a world that had already seen a great deal of horrific devastation (Rhodes 1986). The Manhattan Project was born.

When President Roosevelt died on April 16, 1945, Harry Truman had no knowledge of the highly secret project to develop the atomic bomb. He had met with FDR privately on only two occasions prior to FDR's death. At no time was the atom bomb project or anything else of significance discussed at those meetings, according to Truman's memoirs. Secretary of War Stimson had briefly mentioned that he needed to discuss something very important with him on the day Truman was sworn into office. However, it was not until the end of May that Truman was first fully briefed on the Manhattan Project.

On the morning of July 16, 1945, Truman was in Berlin for the Potsdam Conference with British Prime Minister Winston Churchill and Russian dictator Joseph Stalin. He spent most of the day touring the city and witnessed the total devastation that it had experienced from Allied bombs. As Truman would later write in his diary, it was a very depressing experience that brought him to the vivid and stark reality of the war. It wasn't until the evening of July 16 that he was informed that the first atomic bomb, called "the gadget," had been detonated in a New Mexico desert in the early morning hours. This news was another dose of reality. On that date, we humans knew for certain that we could use the energy of the nucleus of an atom to create weapons whose power for destruction was much greater than ever before known or imagined.

The next day, Truman, Churchill, and Stalin sat together at a table and discussed the most important questions that would impact billions of people and nearly every country in the world. Although Truman had agreed in principle to use the bomb against Japan to save lives that would have been lost on both sides, no final decision had been made. At Potsdam, Stalin had agreed to engage his armies in the war against Japan. Truman had at first been relieved by this decision because it meant the United States would have other armies to share the burden of invading the Japanese homeland. He had previously ordered the assemblage of more than one million troops in preparation of the invasion of Japan. Because intelligence reports indicated that the Japanese were determined to fight on their homeland as long as possible, most military estimates were that 250,000 American soldiers would lose their lives in that invasion.

By July 1945, Truman knew very well the effects of mass bombing on population centers. He remembered the outrage of FDR over the Japanese bombing of Shanghai in 1937. He was also aware that we had sent hundreds of B-29s to firebomb Tokyo and other cities in Japan, resulting in the loss of at least 100,000 lives. Truman had also seen the horrors of war firsthand as an artillery officer during World War I.

The final decision to use the bomb against Japan was made by Truman on June 1, after he was told the decision by a select committee member James Byrnes that they had decided to approve the use of the bomb against Japan (Rhodes 1986, 651). It had long been a foregone conclusion that it would be used. Even at that point in time, the implications of the bomb were seen clearly. The most important and immediate implication for everyone was the prospect of an immediate end to the war and saving hundreds of thousands of lives. In his report on the Trinity test, General Groves stated, "Everyone knew the awful potentialities of the thing that they thought was about to happen . . . the explosion produced a searing light and a roar which warned of doomsday" (AHF 2022).

On August 6, 1945, at 8:15 a.m., the first atomic bomb used in war exploded in an immense fireball above the city of Hiroshima, Japan:

In a city of 250,000, nearly 100,000 people had been killed or doomed at one blow; 100,000 more were hurt. At least 10,000 of the wounded made their way to the best hospital in town, which was altogether unequal to such a trampling. . . . The eyebrows of some were burned off and skin hung from their faces and hands. Others, because of pain, held their arms up as if carrying something in both hands. Some were vomiting as they walked. Many were naked or in shreds of clothing . . . the burns had made patterns—of undershirt straps and suspenders and, on the skin of some women (since white repelled the heat from the bomb and dark clothes absorbed it and conducted it to the skin), the shapes of flowers they had had on their kimonos. (Hersey 1946, 1, 29)

Ultimately, more than 200,000 Japanese lost their lives as a result of the nuclear bombing of the cities of Hiroshima and Nagasaki. These bombings clearly demonstrated the massive and immediate destruction of human lives. As a result of using these terrible weapons, a war was ended but the threat of a war of unimaginable destruction was just beginning.

THE CONCEPT OF NUCLEAR DETERRENCE

"We can't stand another global war. We can't ever have another war, unless it is total war, and that means the end of our civilization, as we know it. We are not going to do that. We are going to accept that Golden Rule and we are going forward to meet our destiny which I think Almighty God intended us to have."
—PRESIDENT HARRY S. TRUMAN, 1945
(MCCULLOUGH 1992, 472)

If anyone in the US government thought that the secrets of the atom bomb could be safeguarded so that no other country could use this nuclear power, that idea was quickly discarded when it was discovered that the Russians had spied on and acquired valuable information during our secret bomb development project. In the fall of 1949, the USSR successfully tested its first nuclear weapon. As many had predicted, the "atomic bomb" was no longer the exclusive property of the United States. These weapons now were the responsibility of humanity as a whole. Once the Soviets had the bomb, it was obvious to Truman what his policy had to be. A declassified National Security Council memorandum (NSC-68) outlining US policy regarding nuclear weapons in 1950 states in part:

> *4. For the moment our atomic retaliatory capability is probably adequate to deter the Kremlin from a deliberate direct military attack against ourselves or other free peoples. However, when it calculates that it has a sufficient atomic capability to make a surprise attack on us, nullifying our atomic superiority and creating a military situation decisively in its favor, the Kremlin might be tempted to strike swiftly and with stealth. The existence of two large atomic capabilities in such a relationship might well act, therefore, not as a deterrent, but as an incitement to war.*

> *5. A further increase in the number and power of our atomic weapons is necessary in order to assure the effectiveness of any U.S. retaliatory blow, but would not of itself seem to change the basic logic of the above points. Greatly increased general air, ground and sea strength, and increased air defense and civilian defense programs, would also be necessary to provide reasonable assurance that the free world could survive an initial surprise atomic attack of the weight which it is estimated the USSR will be capable of delivering by*

1954 and still permit the free world to go on to the eventual attainment of its objectives. Furthermore, such a build-up of strength could safeguard and increase our retaliatory power, and thus might put off for some time the date when the Soviet Union could calculate that a surprise blow would be advantageous. This would provide additional time for the effects of our policies to produce a modification of the Soviet system. (NSC-68 1950, ch. VIII, pt. A)

In retrospect, we can now see some fallacies in this reasoning.

The analysis identifies the USSR as a nuclear superpower that is a clear and present danger to the security of the United States and its allies in the form of nuclear war. This certainly was a reasonable assumption because the Soviets had just taken control of an eastern bloc of nations and had nuclear weapons. However, it goes further by indicating that, if the USSR had nuclear weapons superiority, it would likely take advantage of the situation by attacking us with nuclear weapons! This clear implication set the "hair-trigger" of a potential nuclear war and the urgent necessity of avoiding such a situation. Therefore, the only posture that seemed logical in this calculus was to maintain nuclear weapons superiority or equivalence with the USSR in order to "assure the effectiveness of any U.S. retaliatory blow." This posture would initiate the nuclear arms race. The result, as history has shown, would be the production and stockpile of nuclear weapons and the means of delivering them.

A further result of the arms race was that the possibility of an accidental launch or either side giving serious consideration to their use was significantly increased. Whereas the first assumption seems a logical and conservative one to make, the second was not. By this time, most analysts, including Truman, understood that a nuclear war was not winnable, and a massive nuclear war was not survivable. It would be unlike any war ever fought. The logic that began the nuclear arms race was critically flawed. These two assumptions would create a world living on the razor's edge of doomsday.

Further, our arms race with the USSR would eventually lead to the desire of other nations to possess nukes in search of their own security and ambitions. Finally, the analysis posits that by engaging in this nuclear arms race, the West would have time to "produce a modification of the Soviet system." That logic seems to follow the idea that Stalin was a dictator who could not live forever and that Communism was so flawed that it would eventually self-destruct and the USSR would then follow a more reasonable course. That logic seems now, as it must have seemed then, very naïve and simply wishful thinking. We now understand that the possession of the most potent weapons ever known had some sort of irresistible appeal and a means for any nation to show the world that "we too possess this ultra-power." The dictator Stalin would die and the USSR would dissolve, but the seductive appeal of nuclear weapons would not die.

By 1958, during the Eisenhower administration, the concept of nuclear deterrence had been established. It was defined in a memo from National Security Advisor Robert Cutler to Secretary of State John Foster Dulles. In his summary of conclusions, with respect to nuclear weapons, he stated:

- "All-out war is obsolete as an instrument for the attainment of national objectives. The purpose of a capability for all-out war is to deter its use by an enemy, but once a stalemate of such capabilities has been achieved, to perpetuate it at minimum loss of other capabilities.

- Strategic strength is not usable strength for stable deterrence of, or reply to, minor aggression.

- The U.S. should determine, establish, and maintain the *minimum invulnerable* strategic forces adequate to deter initiation of all-out war by a *rational* opponent" (Cutler 1958).

To paraphrase this policy: a) Nuclear war is obsolete (insane); b) nuclear weapons cannot be used in any conflict; c) we must continue to maintain nuclear weapons superiority/equivalence in order to keep a "reasonable" actor from starting a nuclear war. Again, although assumptions (a) and (b) are reasonable, (c) is a superficial and flawed rationalization. First, it presumes that those who possess nukes would always be rational. It does not consider the possibility that irrational actors would gain access to nukes. It does not consider the fact that other nations would also want to have nukes to deter nations that have them from attacking. History has shown that the policy of nuclear deterrence has not kept us safer from nuclear war but has increased the risk of such a war.

I consider the following to be fatal flaws in the concept of "nuclear deterrence."

- It is grossly irresponsible to have such massively destructive power in our military arsenals, since it would allow military leaders to consider their potential use in war as has been shown by history.

- It has not deterred other nations from acquiring their own nuclear deterrence force and has thereby expanded the nuclear arms race. This has created a greater risk of their use in regional conflicts.

- Reliance on deterrence does not encourage nations of the world toward the objective of the abolition of nuclear weapons. Treaties reducing the number of nuclear weapons remain unsigned by nuclear nations and have not lowered the threshold of nuclear stockpiles below the number that could result in the total destruction of our civilization.

- As a result of nuclear nations maintaining their arsenals, the threat of nuclear war has continued to create fear and instability among those nations. This has resulted in the costly commitments for more and diverse delivery vehicles, weapons modernization, and defining national security around nuclear weaponry.

- The greater number of nuclear nations increases the risk of accidents, theft, or misinterpretation of the intentions of other nuclear nations creating scenarios for "First Use" (a nation decides to strike a nuclear blow before it is attacked).

- For nuclear nations, there is no peaceful alternative to deterrence. If the concept of deterrence is seen as a failed one—due to an instance where a device is used in a conflict, for example—there is no fail-safe position. Retaliation, escalation, and probable nuclear warfare would follow.

Between 1960 and 1967, the world saw the highest rate of increase of nuclear weapons stockpiles. That stockpile doubled from twenty thousand to forty thousand. It was clear to the most disinterested observer that the nuclear arms race was resulting in a world headed for nuclear war.

NUCLEAR CRISES AVERTED

Since Truman, many US presidents have considered using the bomb. All presidents since Truman have had to deal with the threat of nuclear proliferation and thereby the increasing risk of nuclear war. Consider the following documented incidents:

General MacArthur requested of Truman the use of nuclear weapons against China if their troops crossed the Yalu River during the Korean War. In April 1954, Eisenhower offered France two nuclear bombs to use in their war in Vietnam. In September 1954, the US Joint Chiefs of Staff (JCS) recommended using atomic bombs on China over the conflict between Taiwan and China over the islands of Quemoy and Matsu (Pincus 2008).

In 1962, during the Cuban Missile Crisis, the United States under President Kennedy very nearly went to war with the USSR over this confrontation. The new Minuteman I nuclear missile system had the capability of delivering these weapons very quickly. The first MM I squadron was activated on an emergency basis during this crisis, and we reached DEFCON 2 (armed forces are ready to deploy and engage in less than six hours). Because they were both strong nuclear powers, there is little doubt each side could have eventually used its nuclear weapons.

During the Vietnam War, in late January 1968, General Westmoreland warned his superiors that if the situation near the demilitarized zone (DMZ) and at Khe Sanh worsened drastically, nuclear or chemical weapons would have to be used. General McConnell then pressed for Joint Chiefs of Staff authority to prepare a plan for using nuclear weapons to prevent a catastrophic loss of the Marine base. Lyndon Johnson made it clear to his commanders that he did not want to suffer the same kind of defeat as the French had at Diem Bien Phu in 1954. It was only after Johnson was assured that superior air power would protect the base that he took the use of nuclear weapons off the table (Nalty, n.d.).

Richard Nixon twice considered the nuclear option. In 1969, a member of the president's National Security Council (NSC) reported that he had been shown plans that targeted at least two sites in North Vietnam for nuclear air bursts. In 1972, the nuclear option was again considered by Nixon. He told Kissinger that he favored using a nuclear bomb as an alternative to bombing North Vietnam's dike system.

President Gerald Ford had to deal with the attempt to acquire nuclear weapons by Taiwan, India, and Pakistan.

President Jimmy Carter had to deal with the question of a test of a nuclear weapon in South Africa and the possible involvement of Israel in September 1979. Interestingly, Rabin of Israel and South African President Vorster made an agreement to exchange nuclear materials in 1977. Vorster had been imprisoned during World War II for being a Nazi sympathizer, but apparently the lure of nuclear weapons transcended hatred for ex-Nazi sympathizers. Israel had been working to acquire nuclear weapons since 1960 and by 1986 was known to possess them (Richelson 2006, 361). Carter also had to deal with the nuclear weapons testing by India.

President Ronald Reagan had to deal with Libya's and Pakistan's attempts to acquire nuclear weapons. He threatened Pakistan with grave consequences if they continued on the nuclear weapons program. He also had to deal with the nuclear ambitions of Iraq, Iran, and Taiwan. In addition, he had to deal with major nuclear treaty noncompliance issues by the USSR.

President George H. W. Bush had to deal with the reality that both Pakistan and India had nuclear weapons, and that Iraq had an active nuclear weapons program. The US commitment to the Persian Gulf War was, in part, motivated by the threat of Iraq's nuclear program. However, at the end of this war, in March 1991, the Iraqi nuclear program was dismantled under UN supervision.

President Bill Clinton had to deal with the continuation of weapons testing by France, Russia, India, and Pakistan in violation of the Comprehensive Test Ban Treaty (CTBT). He also had to deal with the sale of quantities of uranium ore to "rogue" states.

President George W. Bush wrongly concluded that Iraq had a nuclear weapons program and started another war with Iraq using that erroneous rationale. He also had to deal with the fact that North Korea had indeed developed a nuclear weapons program.

President Barack Obama had to deal with a nuclear North Korea and the threat of nukes in Iran. These could certainly be considered rogue states and capable of selling weapons or weapons technology to extremist factions.

TOWARD ZERO NUKES

On October 7, 1963, JFK signed the Limited Test Ban Treaty with the USSR, prohibiting nuclear testing in the atmosphere.

In 1968, the United Nations produced the Non-Proliferation Treaty (NPT). The preamble to the treaty offered these statements of hope for the future of humankind:

> *Considering the devastation that would be visited upon all mankind by a nuclear war and the consequent need to make every effort to avert the danger of such a war, and to take measures to safeguard the security of peoples,*

> *Believing that the proliferation of nuclear weapons would seriously enhance the danger of nuclear war, . . .*

> *Declaring their intention to achieve at the earliest possible date the cessation of the nuclear arms race and to undertake effective measures in the direction of nuclear disarmament, . . .*

> *Desiring to further the easing of international tension and the strengthening of trust between States in order to facilitate the cessation of the manufacture of nuclear weapons, the liquidation of all their existing stockpiles, and the elimination from national arsenals of nuclear weapons and the means of their delivery pursuant to a Treaty on general and complete disarmament under strict and effective international control, . . .*

> *Have agreed . . . (United Nations 1968)*

The United States and Russia signed the treaty on July 1, 1968. The four nonsignatories to the NPT (India, Pakistan, North Korea, and Israel) have nuclear weapons.

On May 26, 1972, SALT I, the first agreement to limit the number and types of nuclear weapons, was signed by Nixon and Brezhnev.

On December 8, 1987, Reagan and Gorbachev signed the Intermediate Range Nuclear Forces Treaty (INF), thereby eliminating an entire class of nuclear weapons.

In September 1996, the UN-sponsored Comprehensive Test Ban Treaty (CTBT) was open for signatures. The treaty would ban all nuclear weapons testing. To date, all but eight countries have ratified it. The United States is among the eight nations that have not yet ratified the treaty. Although the UN treaty has no enforcement power, through contributions from member states, it has established a strong verification regimen. It is a $1 billion investment that is able to detect any nuclear explosion anywhere in the world.

On May 24, 2002, the United States and Russia signed the Strategic Offensive Reductions Treaty (SORT). The treaty requires that "each Party shall reduce and limit strategic nuclear warheads . . . so that by Dec. 31, 2012, the aggregate number of such warheads does not exceed 1,700 to 2,200 for each Party. Each Party shall determine for itself the composition and structure of its strategic offensive arms, based on the established aggregate limit for the number of such warheads" ("New START Treaty" 2010; CRS 2011).

The New START Treaty between the United States and Russia was signed on April 8, 2010, and ratified in February 2011. The treaty limits the aggregate number of deployed warheads to 1,550 for each country. Warheads on deployed ICBMs (intercontinental ballistic missiles) and deployed SLBMs (submarine-launched ballistic missiles) count toward this limit, and each deployed heavy bomber equipped for nuclear armaments counts as one warhead toward this limit. The limit is 74 percent lower than the limit of the 1991 START Treaty and 30 percent lower than the deployed strategic warhead limit of the 2002 Moscow Treaty.

As a result of this treaty, the United States and Russia have entered into an unprecedented era of cooperation on nuclear weapons. By December 2011, each country had conducted eighteen audits of the other nation's nuclear sites. The treaty calls for the nations to regularly share quantities, siting, and schematics of armament equipment and sites. The sides to date have swapped more than 1,800 notifications under the treaty. The United States has also demonstrated to Russia that the B-1B bomber can no longer carry nuclear weapons.

Aside from the threat of nuclear war, there have been many incidents involving radioactive materials that had or could have had serious implications to human and environmental health.

ACCIDENTAL EMISSIONS

Three Mile Island

Three Mile Island, on March 28, 1979, was the worst accident in US commercial nuclear power plant history and resulted in the release of small amounts of radioactive gases and radioactive iodine into the environment. The Nuclear Regulatory Commission's (NRC) authorization of the release of 40,000 gallons (about 150,000 liters) of radioactive wastewater directly in the Susquehanna River resulted in a public outcry over the safety of nuclear power facilities (Omang 1979).

Chernobyl

On April 26, 1986, a nuclear core meltdown occurred at Unit 4 of the nuclear power station at Chernobyl, Ukraine, in what was then USSR. The accident, caused by a sudden surge of power, destroyed the reactor and released massive amounts of radioactive material into the environment. The population that was evacuated from the most heavily contaminated areas numbered approximately 115,000 in 1986 and another 220,000 people in subsequent years (United Nations 2008).

Nuclear Cruise Missiles

On August 30, 2007, during the transfer of some advanced cruise missiles (ACM) from Minot Air Force Base in North Dakota, six ACMs with nuclear warheads still installed were mistakenly loaded onto a B-52 and flown across the United States to Barksdale Air Force Base in Louisiana, where they sat on the tarmac unattended for more than a day (Spencer, Ludin, and Nelson 2012).

Nuclear Submarine Fire

On December 29, 2011, Russia came close to nuclear disaster when a blaze engulfed a nuclear-powered submarine that was carrying nuclear weapons. During the fire, the submarine was carrying sixteen R-29 intercontinental ballistic missiles, each armed with four nuclear warheads (Faulconbridge 2012).

Fukushima

On March 11, 2011, a 9.0 magnitude earthquake and resulting forty-nine-foot tsunami hit Japan near the Fukushima-Daiichi nuclear power facility. The damage to the nuclear facility from this incident was a series of equipment failures, reactor meltdown, and the release of radioactive materials into the surrounding ecosphere. This clearly was one of the worst nuclear disasters in history, and effects of the radiological damage from this incident are still being felt. This disaster significantly impacted the world's use of nuclear reactors to generate electrical power, with many countries shutting down their nuclear generators.

Hanford Nuclear Fuel Plant

From 1943 until 1971, the nuclear processing plant near Hanford, Washington, was cooled by water from the Columbia River. Millions of gallons of water were pumped directly through reactor cores and picked up enormous quantities of nuclear material, making the Columbia River downstream the most radioactive river in the world. The disastrous leaching of radioactive materials into the ground around the Hanford nuclear site near the Columbia River resulted in a high incidence of thyroid cancer in the nearby towns.

In 1986, the US government finally admitted to secretly releasing the radiation into the environment without informing the public that it had done so or the health hazards involved. "A $27 million government study concluded in 1990 that the releases (of radiation) had put people at risk for developing thyroid disease, triggering the litigation" (Reynolds 2002, 1046–1048).

Radiological Thermal Generators (RTGs)

In the mid-1950s, the concept of generating electricity from the release of thermal energy from radioactivity was put into practice with the development of these portable devices. With little fanfare or public knowledge, RTGs were placed aboard spacecraft to provide a low-weight, reliable, electrical power source. The first launch of RTGs into space came in 1961. On April 21, 1964, when the US–built Transit-5BN-3 navigational satellite failed to achieve orbit, its RTG power source disintegrated in the atmosphere and released its seventeen thousand curies of radiation. This release tripled the worldwide environmental inventory of plutonium-238 and increased the total world environmental burden (measured in curies) from all plutonium isotopes by about 4 percent.

One of the most serious accidents occurred in 1978 when booster failure during the launch of the Russian satellite Cosmos 854 resulted in the premature reentry of the reactor on board. As a result of this accident, radioactive debris was scattered over northwest Canada. Some of this debris was found to be highly radioactive. Since RTGs have been in use, there has been a significant history of accidents involving the release of radioactive materials (Aftergood 1989). RTGs are still very much in use in space missions. We know, however, that some of the applications will remain classified.

THE YIN AND YANG OF NUCLEAR DETERRENCE

It is true that since the first use of the atom bomb in war, there have been no nuclear attacks by any nation against another. However, as documented, we have flirted with that possibility many times. Though we can claim that having nuclear weapons has made it clear that the prospect of having a nuclear war is unimaginable, and therefore kept the world of nations from entering into such a war, we must also face the fact that other countries have used the same rationale to develop their own nuclear arsenal. Therefore, because some countries do have nukes and thus pose a threat to others, we effectively ensure that we will have a world where there will be nuclear weapons proliferation. The reasonable ultimate conclusion to this escalation of nukes is that the more nukes there are in the world, the greater the risk of nuclear war.

The concept of eliminating nuclear war by maintaining a stout arsenal of nuclear weapons is a flawed rationale because, in practical terms, it increases the probability that the thing we are trying to prevent will happen. This is a very simple calculus that anyone can understand. We humans are warlike. Our history has been that we don't have long periods of peace without warfare. The rationale of using any weapon in war to save lives was established from the beginning of warfare.

Therefore, our capacity to rationalize the use of these weapons in future wars already exists in the minds of presidents and generals. The enormous destructive power of these weapons is such that, if we were convinced that we would soon be attacked by nukes, we would not have the time to hesitate in deciding whether to strike first. In fact, US policy has never rejected the possibility of a nuclear first strike.

President Kennedy concluded that the nuclear superpowers were in a "nuclear stalemate." He further stated that preemption "was not possible for us" (Burr and Rosenberg 2010, 90–91). Both sides would have to be even more careful than they had been in the past if they were to avoid catastrophe. Nevertheless, the US war plan would continue to include preemptive options in the unlikely event that decision-makers had strategic warning of an impending Soviet attack. We remained on the nuclear precipice.

Throughout his tenure in office, President George W. Bush had a policy that allowed for a preemptive nuclear strike (US Department of Defense 2005). The current US policy on the use of nuclear weapons is stated in the Defense Department manual. Section 2-7 reads:

> *The United States may use nuclear weapons to terminate a conflict or war at the lowest acceptable level of hostilities. The employment of nuclear weapons by the United States is governed by guidance to the joint force commander as contained in strategic-level directives. The United States is party to treaties and international agreements that limit proliferation, testing and possession of nuclear weapons. ("Multi-Service Doctrine" 2011, 2-2)*

This is purposely worded in vague terms to allow wide latitude for the use of nukes. What does "terminate a conflict or war at the lowest acceptable level of hostilities" mean? If the United States considers a threat to use weapons of mass destruction (WMDs) against us the beginning of a conflict, then it could be interpreted to mean that we can use nuclear weapons before the other side takes any action (i.e., a preemptive strike). We can conclude that our current policy is that we maintain the option to use nuclear weapons when we deem it necessary. Preemptive strike is still an integral part of the policy of nuclear deterrence that has been with us from the beginning of the nuclear age.

Actually, you could argue that the concept of preemptive strike is derived from the primordial law of the jungle: kill or be killed. What we need to recognize is that we are trying to evolve to more sentient, holistic beings that think, analyze, and contemplate and more carefully consider the results of our actions. The "moral" impediment to using nukes for the complete and total destruction of massive numbers of people during wartime has already been established by our history with war. Let us pause and consider that for a moment. Somehow, we humans think that the mass murder of other humans can be justified. Is that concept now a part of our human moral code? Must it be so? I think it is a moral cancer that needs to be removed.

HOW WOULD WE ACCOUNT FOR OUR STEWARDSHIP OF PLANET EARTH?

Former Secretary of Defense Robert Gates concluded that Russia would not be able to achieve "militarily significant cheating" under the New START Treaty. The treaty does not preclude the enhancement of safety, security, reliability, or modernization of nuclear weapons stockpiles. It also does not restrict the deployment of anti-ballistic missile systems ("New START Treaty" 2011; CRS 2010).

However, the question of the political will of the major powers to work diligently to reach zero nukes remains. At the present time, we seem to have settled on the total of 1,550 nuclear weapons each. Why 1,550? Is this the minimum number of nukes that would be required to deliver a devastating retaliatory blow to the other nation?

Obviously the issue of trust in the integrity of the other nation to carry out its treaty responsibility is still a concern. We still have to prove to each other that the verification protocol works. This will involve disclosure and trust. The fact that we have different political and social institutions may keep us from achieving this level of trust.

How do we get to that level?

In my opinion, we can achieve a high level of trust though mutual acceptance and recognition that we have common objectives. This must be a focus of the foreign policies of both major nuclear powers, not an afterthought. In order to reach that point, the political arguments must be made convincingly so that no party disagrees. It is not enough to simply declare this as a policy of the current administration. There must be open and honest dialogue. This, of course, has been missing from US politics because the dialogue has been divisive and dogmatic on most issues. However, the arguments to be made are there:

- The expense is staggering.

- Nuclear materials continue to pile up at an increasing rate.

- The problem of nuclear waste disposal is increasing.

- Weapons proliferation is worsening and more independent nations want access to nuclear technology.

- Therefore the threat of a nuclear incident is increasing.

- The threat of nuclear warfare is increasing and our civilization as we know it is at stake.

These arguments are compelling. We just need strong leaders of the major nuclear powers to make them with a sense of urgency.

It should be recognized that the New START agreement between the United States and Russia is only one part of myriad actions that need to be pursued if we are to minimize the risk of nuclear proliferation. Although success with New START will be a significant and important model for how cooperation between the two largest nuclear powers can be achieved, we still have to deal with the other nuclear powers. As of this writing, there are nine countries that possess nuclear weapons: the United States, the UK, France, Russia, China, Israel, India, Pakistan, and North Korea. It is safe to say that some of these countries have made serious threats of war against each other. The fact that this many countries possess and have the ability to produce these nuclear weapons also confirms the reality that there are really no secrets when it comes to their production. The ways and means to construct them is available to any country (or group) that wants them.

The reality is that the knowledge, capability, and technology to harness the energy of the atom are well understood worldwide. In 1945, these were the highest and most closely held secrets in the world. But today, the knowledge needed to refine uranium ore (yellowcake) to "enriched" U-235 is readily available. Actual construction of a fission bomb would certainly be a technical challenge but not an impossible one, as has been shown by the North Korean nuclear weapons tests. Therefore, we find ourselves in the situation in which the capability to build nuclear weapons is available to any nation, access to radioactive material is available to any nation, and the technical knowledge and equipment to enrich uranium are available to any nation.

In addition, rational nations have concluded that the use of nuclear weapons in war is unimaginable if we are to survive as a civilization. We are left with only one way to deal with countries that aspire to obtain nuclear weapons. The use of diplomatic negotiations and nonviolent confrontation with countries like Iran and North Korea, such as the use of economic sanctions, is not only the correct approach, it may also be the only viable approach.

As we have noted from a review of current Defense Department policies regarding weapons of mass destruction, military action against a nation threatening the use of WMDs is still an option. However, if we were to engage in military actions against nation states to avoid proliferation, we must consider that the end effect could well be an escalation of hostilities involving other nations with WMDs. Then, a further result would likely be that the concept of peaceful disarmament would be negated, and we would all return to nuclear-armed camps.

Clearly, the international community of nations and people must work closely and diligently together if we are to eventually solve the nuclear weapons problem. After the almost eighty years since the first nuclear test at the Trinity site in New Mexico, this responsibility is still collectively ours, and the implications of the immediate and complete destruction that could result from their use are vivid and undeniable. There is no turning back, or turning our backs on the nuclear issue. We have no choice but to deal with it.

In fact, it may be that the invention of the atomic bomb was necessary for our evolving human consciousness. Certainly, human evolution does not occur in a cosmic vacuum. We are made of "star stuff": We are part of an organized sun system that is part of a bigger galaxy of systems, and our galaxy is only a small part of a universe of galaxies. There may well be universal reasons why we invented nuclear weapons. Our own evolutionary consciousness and how we relate to the universe of consciousness may well be one of those reasons.

UFOS AND NUCLEAR WEAPONS

The late, great cosmologist Carl Sagan wrote:

> *How would we explain the global arms race to a dispassionate extraterrestrial observer? . . . Would we argue that 10,000 targeted nuclear warheads are likely to enhance the prospects for our survival? What account would we give of our stewardship of the planet Earth? We have heard the rationales offered by the nuclear superpowers. We know who speaks for the nations. But who speaks for the human species? Who speaks for Earth? (Sagan [1980] 2013, 347)*

Sagan was publicly skeptical about the reality of the UFO phenomenon because he claimed that the available evidence was not sufficient to take that position. However, in his book *Cosmos*, his position on the possibility of alien civilizations is self-evident: "All my life I have wondered about the possibility of life elsewhere. . . . And on some small fraction of worlds there may develop intelligences and civilizations more advanced than our own" (Sagan [1980] 2013, 17–18).

To date, many former or retired US Air Force personnel—once trusted to operate or guard weapons of mass destruction—have come forward and revealed ongoing UFO surveillance of, and occasional interference with, our nuclear weapons. The entire body of these factual accounts alters the historical perspective on the nuclear arms race. Following is an abbreviated listing of some of these incidents. The fact that the Pentagon and CIA have successfully kept the truth from the public for so long is also an aspect of this phenomenon.

The Connection between UFOs and Nuclear Weapons

1945	UFOs chased by Navy pilots over Hanford, WA, nuclear fuel processing plant before the first atomic bomb test; witness Lieutenant Bud Clem, USN
1947	UFOs crash near Roswell Army Air Force Base, NM, home of the 509th Bomber Group, the only atomic bomber base in the United States where nuclear bombs were stored
1950s	Multiple UFO sightings near the early nuclear tests at Nevada proving grounds near Yucca Flats, NV
1959	Beale AFB, CA, a B-52 nuclear bomber base: multiple UFO sightings and chases of UFOs by Air Force interceptors over the base; witness John Mullican

1962	Ramey AFB, Puerto Rico: During the Cuban Missile Crisis, UFOs overflew B-52 base during a period when the United States was in DEFCON 2; a period closest to war with the USSR
1963	Walker AFB, NM (previously Roswell AFB): UFOs seen over Atlas Missile Launch Facility; witnesses Lieutenant Jerry Nelson and others
1964	Vandenberg AFB, CA: videotape of UFO flying around nose cone of an Atlas missile during test flight over Pacific Test Range; CIA confiscated video; witnesses Lieutenant Robert Jacobs and Major Mansmann
1967	Malmstrom AFB, MT—Minuteman Missile Base: UFOs shut down twenty nuclear missiles over a span of a week; witnesses Lieutenant Robert Salas, Lieutenant Walt Figel, and many others
1968	Minot AFB, ND—Minuteman Missile Base: UFOs seen over Missile Launch Control Center; caused disruption in electronics systems and communication; report that the twenty-ton cover over the Launch Facility was removed during the UFO encounter; witnesses Major Bradford Runyon and others
1976	Ellsworth AFB, SD: UFO hovered over Launch Control Center and disrupted missile operations; security guards fired 180 rounds of ammunition at the object with no effect; witnesses interrogated using extreme methods
1979	Aviano AFB, Italy, a US/NATO base with tactical nuclear weapons: UFO hovered near the weapons storage area causing electronic interference
1979	Soesterberg AFB, Netherlands, a US/NATO base with tactical nuclear weapons: UFO flew down the flight line for extended period; witnesses Josie Zwinenberg and many others

1980	Bentwaters Base, UK, a US/NATO base: UFOs observed over three nights; UFO shone a beam of light near weapons storage area; witnesses interrogated with extreme measures by intelligence agents; witnesses Colonel Charles Halt, Airman Larry Warren, and many others
2010	F. E. Warren AFB, WY: Air Force personnel observed large UFO during shutdown of fifty Minuteman missiles; witnesses: many USAF and civilian persons

Though most of the reported UFO incursions apparently involved simple observation, a few resulted in the shutdown of large numbers of nuclear missiles. This is more than a Cold War issue, because these incidents continue to occur. Nuclear weapons proliferation is an ominous and crucial concern that affects not only the human civilization but has also been shown to be an obvious concern for extraterrestrial civilizations.

THE WORLD SET FREE

"The moral shock of the atomic bombs had been a profound one, and for a while the cunning side of the human animal was overpowered by its sincere realization of the vital necessity for reconstruction. . . . I suppose that nothing less than the violence of those bombs could have released it and made it a healthy world again. I suppose they were necessary."
—H. G. WELLS, *THE WORLD SET FREE*
([1914] 2015, 106, 116)

In his amazing novel, written many decades before the world had to confront the nuclear arms race, nuclear deterrence, and the possibility of nuclear war, Wells was able to capture the very real questions we face today. If we cannot solve this problem, will we be faced with the devastating answer that in order to move forward together, humankind must suffer the horrors of nuclear war? Is it necessary? Or as Oppenheimer said, "It is not for us to believe that. By our works we are committed, committed to a world united, before this common peril, in law and in humanity" (Bird and Sherwin 2005, 329).

For anyone who will simply take the time to seriously research the facts of UFO sightings, the evidence is overwhelming that we have had extraterrestrial visitors for some time, and at least since the advent of the atomic bomb. And the evidence is also overwhelming that they are trying to shine a light on our nuclear weapons. Their intense and continuing interest in what we humans do with respect to nukes suggests the depth to which they understand our problem. They may have survived their own transition through dealing with their own WMDs. They know that we may or may not be able to avoid a nuclear war. However, if humanity does in fact resolve the nuclear problem, then we can also move confidently forward to try to resolve our other pressing problems, such as global warming and water and food security. These, too, are issues that could devastate the human civilization. I see the extraterrestrial presence as a positive impetus that, if recognized as a positive influence by the public, can help us not only to survive but also allow us to demonstrate to the ETs that we have the will, the intellect, and the character qualities to continue on a peaceful evolutionary path.

CHAPTER 8

ET and Me

"When, for example, one experiencer would be shown
a picture of the aliens drawn by another experiencer,
he or she would react with horror, because that meant
someone else was having the experience and their notion
that they could somehow dismiss this as a dream was
shattered. That response struck me as something that
could only occur if something real, and not imaginary,
had happened to them. Dreams do not work like that.
People do not respond to another's dreams that way. So
something in me said there is something going on here
that I do not understand."

—DR. JOHN MACK (1995, 96–110), PROFESSOR OF
PSYCHIATRY, HARVARD MEDICAL SCHOOL

THE ABDUCTION PHENOMENON

In 1981, Dr. Hopkins published his first book on the
abduction phenomenon. In it, he concluded that ETs
are engaged in "a systematic 'research' program, with the
human species as subject" (Hopkins 1981, 19). He estimated that tens of thousands have been abducted in this

manner. He went on to write, "All I can say is that I'm sure it is going on; people are being picked up, 'examined'—sometimes marked for life—and released; their memories conveniently blocked" (24).

Although Dr. Hopkins has now passed on, other researchers have continued the research and have provided a voice for these abduction experiencers.

Yvonne Smith, a certified hypnotherapist, provides hypnotherapy for abductees and has formed a support group called CERO (Close Encounter Research Organization). In her book *Chosen*, she provides the testimonies of many who have been shown hybrid children that they are told are theirs. She states, "It appears we have entered a 'new phase' of this alien agenda, which deeply involves the 'evolution' of an ongoing hybridization program" (Smith 2008, 209). She and other researchers also suggest that there may very well be hybrids walking among us.

One of the more famous and significant abduction cases is that of Barney and Betty Hill in September 1961. The definitive account of this incident is presented in the book *Captured* by Stanton Friedman and Kathleen Marden (2007). The Hills were abducted, taken aboard a craft, and "examined." Under hypnosis, Betty and Barney later recalled their experience in great detail, even though they were both told by their captors not to reveal anything.

Their sessions were held separately, and their stories showed amazing concurrence of those details. Betty recalls having a (telepathic) conversation with one of her abductors. He showed her a star map that indicated from where they traveled and other star systems they would visit. She was also shown some sort of book with strange writing. She was able to give a precise physical description of these beings. Also of great significance for the purpose of correlation with other descriptions of these objects, she was able to describe the appearance of the UFO craft. Specifically, although the craft initially looked similar to the one described by John Mullican and others, as it left the Hills, the craft looked like an orange fireball, similar to what was described by John Smith; this is also a familiar description by other witnesses. Betty verified the erratic (not smooth) motion of the craft as it flew, which is well supported in many other sightings.

Highly experienced and respected researcher Ann Druffel has also written many books on abductions. In fact she has written a how-to book called *How to Defend Yourself Against Alien Abduction*. That book lists nine resistance techniques that seemed to have worked in attempted abductions. In Druffel's book *The Tujunga Canyon Contacts*, two of the principals involved describe the eerie blue light that preceded the arrival of the aliens. Again, this is a fairly common aspect of these incidents and one that has particular significance to me. One of these abductees claimed she was given some specific information on a simple cure for cancer during her experience. That witness later dedicated much of her working life to healthcare. Essentially all abductees seem to be given information, messages, special abilities, direction, or some special "mission" to perform upon their return. While there is little doubt that some sort of hybridization program is ongoing, there is also little doubt that ETs are trying to somehow "improve" our species.

WHAT DO THEY LOOK LIKE?

From a composite of multiple witness accounts that have been documented, we are getting a better picture of how a typical "gray" ET appeared to abductees.

They are in the range of three and a half to five and a half feet tall. They have large, oval or egg-shaped heads that are disproportionately bigger than their bodies. They are "skinny" and have long arms, although some describe them as fit and strong. Their fingers have been described as long and mechanical looking. Some have described the fingers as being nearly cylindrical. Some have described the finger pads as having small suction cups.

Their skin has been variously described as a chalky-white color or very pale and gray tinged. The skin texture has been described as having the consistency of marshmallow or putty. There is no body hair on their skin. Their eyes have generally been described as large. Some say the eyes are a glassy black, with no pupil discernible, and almond shaped. Others describe the eyes as normal, with pupils, but larger than ours and sweeping back alongside the head. Their apparent ages vary widely, from the very young to the very old. The caveat to some of these observed attributes is that many abductees thought that they were wearing some sort of uniform and mask to hide their true appearance and/or to be able to maneuver in our environment.

THE MESSAGES FROM ETS

For whatever the reasons that these abductions are occurring, the ETs take the opportunity to convey messages to abductees. Communications are telepathic, and many of the messages are intended to be either subliminal or to be fully understood at some later date. Many of the messages seem to encompass the concept that they are very interested in our life forms and want to see us thrive and protect our planet from harm. This essential message also includes the specific admonition that we will not be able to protect our people and our planet and survive as a species unless we learn to live and work together in peace. Abductees have been told this is the main reason the ETs have not been in more direct contact with us.

This is certainly a very ancient message that we have all heard, in one form or another, all of our lives. We have seen it in our holy books, and it has come down to us from the farthest reaches of human history. It is nothing new. The obvious truth is that we as a species have not heeded this essential message well. We continue on a path of doing harm to ourselves and to our home planet. We continue to threaten our very existence with nuclear weapons and other means of mass destruction. However, just as someone who loves us such as our own mothers may say to us, no matter how old we are and what our experiences may be, these are simply messages of concern for our well-being.

Mike and Leo Dworshak were boys of ten and twelve years old when they encountered a UFO near their family farm in North Dakota in 1932. Leo Dworshak wrote about these encounters in his book, *UFOs Are with Us—Take My Word*. He claims to have visited ETs in their ship many times during his life. He wrote that they looked more like us. Their message for humankind as given to him was essentially the same as previously stated: that they do come in peace and are here to monitor our behavior among ourselves. They are, however, mainly concerned with our planet. Of course, those two objectives are intertwined because we are the ones that are in a position to either protect or do damage to this planet.

Leo remembers how kind they were to him and his brother. He felt welcomed like a good friend during each visit. They told him that they would continue traveling to our planet as our world gets in deeper trouble. They spoke about us humans reaching a critical point in our evolution where we would be faced with important decisions regarding our very survival. Although they told him that they are responsible for protecting the planet, they also said that did not guarantee our survival. They communicated telepathically with Leo and seemed to get their messages across within the context of shared emotions. If we think about the times when people have conveyed what we perceive to be their truth, it has been through sensing their true emotions.

The last time Leo visited with these ETs was in 1963 near Ennis, Montana. One of their main messages to him at that time was: "Your science and technology have advanced enough to pose a threat to our ships, as well as to the entire planet" (Dworshak 2003, 68). Leo then added: "A picture of the mushroom cloud following an atomic blast filled my mind" (68). The first Minuteman nuclear missiles become operational in Montana in October 1962.

I must emphasize here that in my own incident in Montana, just before my missiles were disabled and the UFO was still above the front gate to our Launch Control

Center, I vividly recall pausing to look at my status board. I remember getting the distinct communication: *We are going to shut down your nuclear weapons.* I am convinced that I, too, received the same sort of direct communication from an ET as given to Leo Dworshak. I have long since interpreted my experience as one of an admonition that humanity should rid itself of nuclear weapons for the sake of its own survival. It is interesting to note also that Leo and his brother grew up and encountered a UFO near the town of Killdeer, North Dakota, not far from the current location of some of the Minuteman missile sites.

THE PRINCIPLE OF NONINTERFERENCE

Some abductees have been told that their ET visitors to Earth are under a sort of obligation not to interfere with our evolutionary development, in either a positive or negative way. However, there seems to be no restriction to relaying positive messages to give us sustenance and encourage our growth. Abductee Virginia Horton (Hopkins 1981, 128–153) was told this principle has been established as an edict by some sort of intergalactic federation of beings. This principle makes some sense if we relate it to our own behavior toward other countries. Ideally, democratic nations would like to see other countries develop their own form of governance and keep their social identities.

In my study, I have a print made from a painting by Charles M. Russell. The original hangs in the State Capitol Building of Montana. It depicts the first meeting between a tribe of Flathead Native Americans and Lewis and Clark on the plains of Montana. The natives are depicted as being excited that they had made contact with another race of people for the first time, and seems to show them instinctively demonstrating their desire to live in peace with these alien-looking men. To be fair, this could also have been the desire of Lewis and Clark, although they had with them a declaration from President Jefferson stating that he was the natives' "Great White Father" and protector.

This picture both saddens and heartens me. I am saddened to think that the natives did not realize what was to become of them within a short time. As with nearly all other ethnic tribes in the Americas, their future would see them becoming the victims of violence, with the destruction of their social order and religious beliefs, the theft of their lands and social order, discrimination, isolation, and—worst of all—loss of self-esteem. I am heartened by the fact that they seem to be expressing the natural good will of people welcoming strangers to their land. This picture leads me to wonder what kind of emotions and thoughts would transpire between us during a first "we come in peace" meeting between humans and an ET culture. However, it is likely that happened a long time ago. And, as members of an advanced civilization that has encountered many other life forms in their travels and gone through the growing pains of socialization with them, they would likely understand the pitfalls of those interactions.

At this point, I accept the likelihood that the "principle of noninterference," with the possible exceptions of nuclear war and other events that could result in mass annihilation of other life forms, has been instituted by ET races visiting our planet. This follows the line of thinking that the ETs may have had a hand in the development and evolution of life on earth. All living organisms are therefore of high importance to them and to all *intelligent* beings in the cosmos. If we continue that line of reasoning, we must conclude that they have indeed "come in peace," by that standard.

THE PROSPECT OF ET DISCLOSURE

A common thread in abductions seems to be that each abductee is given some information about their hosts. Some are shown star fields, shown their propulsion system, given a tour of the ship, shown other ETs at work. Many of the children abductees are also taken to a sort of school where they learn things such as telekinesis and other techniques to develop psychic abilities. Some report "downloads" of technical information. And all abductees are subjected to the deep look into the eyes by the dominant ET being. For many, this deep, long look into their eyes felt like they were being told something, but they knew that they would not be able to remember or process that information for a period of time.

Abductions seem to be a way for ETs to communicate with humans on a very personal level. It doesn't matter what politicians say or do about this phenomenon: The ETs may have their own means of disclosing to the world human population the truth about themselves. It is interesting to note that although virtually all abductees are told they are not allowed to remember what they have seen and the information and knowledge they are given, there will come a time when they will remember and will be able to speak in depth about this knowledge.

THE DOCTOR WILL SEE YOU NOW

Why continue to give abductees physical examinations? It is certainly not due to curiosity about human anatomy or physiology. ETs already know about basic human physiology because they have probably been interacting with humankind for thousands of years or more. It is therefore likely they want to see how we are changing physically, intellectually, ethically, psychologically, and in other ways as a result of our evolutionary journey. Evolution for us is a complex affair. We humans are undergoing evolutionary changes at the same time we are making rapid changes in technology. There is also the consideration of genetic mutations that are happening to us as a result of environmental and adaptational changes.

Could it be that they want to gauge the general health of our species? Do they want to be able to estimate our chances for survival? Are we evolving well enough to be a "successful" life form in this galaxy and in the universe of galaxies? If you were making a judgment about the prospects for our survival, what would you say?

ANTHROPOLOGIC GENETICS

In *Chosen*, an abductee named John relates: "They're telling me to have feelings for this baby (he sees a baby with an umbilical cord in a tank of some fluid). That it is mine. I don't know if it's mine, they're telling me to love it. They're telling me to feel love for that baby" (Smith 2008, 81). Yvonne Smith, who has dealt with many such abductees, writes, "there are hundreds of cases of people who have had similar experiences like John's. They are presented with children who, they are told, were theirs" (81). Could it be that ETs seem to understand the importance of the love bonding between parent and child for the optimal growth and development of the child?

Other witnesses talk of seeing hybrid (human/ET) embryos or holding hybrid babies. What can we conclude from these brief insights? I think this evidence, and it is evidence, shows that, for whatever other reasons they may have for being here, the ETs (or some of them) are involved in a hybridization program with humans and they want to have or produce a closer relationship with humanity.

The ETs must have studied human nature for a long time. They must know our tendencies very well, including our preoccupation with sex.

It would be interesting to speculate how they are manipulating our genes and for what purposes.

We could very well be the result of an experiment that was started a long time ago with our ancient predecessors. At what point did they start manipulating life forms? Were they here at the very inception of life on this planet? If so, have they started experiments on other planets? Who are they and where did they originate? The questions are many, and run deep.

MY MEETING WITH ETS

In 1985, I was living in Manhattan Beach, California, with my wife, Marilyn, and our two children in a home I was remodeling. It was one of many homes I would buy and remodel in Manhattan Beach during the fifteen years we lived in that city. I recall the specific location and the general layout of the house.

One evening, long after we had all gone to sleep, I awoke suddenly and noticed a light coming from our living room. I woke Marilyn and she, too, saw the light. I was very anxious about this because I thought someone must have broken into our home. I told Marilyn I would investigate. The light was a strange color of blue and seemed to be drifting into our bedroom. As I tried to get out of bed, I found myself paralyzed and could not move my arms or legs. I could move my head, and I turned to face Marilyn to ask for help. I was amazed to realize that she had gone back to sleep. I struggled as hard as I could to try to regain movement in my limbs but to no avail. I felt helpless. Next, I noticed a figure in our bedroom doorway and also felt there were others in our bedroom. I only recall the outline of the figure in the doorway. The figure was dark or had dark clothes on, and seemed to have a hood over its head. I do not recall the appearance of the face.

What I remember happening next was amazing. I received a message that I would be moving toward the window. Indeed, I was lifted off my bed and started floating toward the window that faced our backyard. As I was moving toward the window, I recall looking down at my unconscious wife. I also had the thought that "they" would not be able to open the window because they didn't know how the latch worked. Now, I find this amusing.

The next thing I remember is being on the other side of that window. This is where my memory of the next sequence of events fails me. However, I do recall that some sort of procedure was performed on me (apparently in the craft). I remember being shown a very long, needle-like instrument. I was informed (telepathically) that the needle would be inserted into my groin and that it would not hurt. However, as they began to insert this needle, I recall feeling extreme pain. When I complained about the pain, the pain was relieved. I do not remember anything else specific to that event.

However, at times over the years, I have had bits of memories come forward—usually during dreams or semi-conscious states of mind. For example, I recall seeing a large, black, oval eyeball very close to my face. This was so clear that I could see the glassy texture of the eye and even the skin surrounding the perimeter of the eye. I also remember seeing a "doctor" dressed in black, opening and rummaging through a box of instruments. I once had a dream/vision of seeing a kind of stream of technical symbols and numbers pass through my field of view in a very rapid manner, as though I were being uploaded with some information.

Marilyn, who also recalls the blue light entering our bedroom, insists that my recollection of the door and window location of that room were not of that house but of another house in which we had lived. Therefore, I think it is likely that I (we) had more than one such encounter.

Today, as I write this, I am not sure whether I want to know what else transpired during that event. From what I have read and from the discussions I have had with other abductees, there is such a wide variety of experiences from such encounters and the fact that ETs do have means of projecting "screen memories" or obscuring memories, that it may be very difficult to sort out the true picture of what happened. I have no doubt that I was taken, and that my experience was in many ways "typical" for these ET encounters. I find myself more interested in this question: For what purpose was I, and so many others, taken?

WHAT IS TRUE ABOUT ETS?

We may not have all the answers, but from the body of work from researchers and the testimonies of witnesses, we can draw some general conclusions:

- They are able to communicate directly to our minds— telepathic communication.
- They have the ability to control or affect the human neurosensory system (i.e., paralysis, pain control).
- They have the ability to affect human memory of events.
- They understand our DNA makeup.
- They have the ability to understand our most technical equipment and concepts (e.g., nuclear weaponry).
- They are involved in an active genetic manipulation or hybridization program.

On the speculative side, this is what I suspect is real:

- They have the ability to fine-tune human abilities to the point of giving us some "special" qualities (i.e., psychic abilities).

- They are manipulating certain abductees through some form of mind control.

- They want to raise the human level of consciousness to improve our species.

- They could very well be here to "train" us to qualify for inclusion in the cosmic community of "intelligent" life.

CHAPTER 9

The Last Country

National boundaries are not evident when we view the Earth from space. Fanatical ethnic or religious or national zeal is a little difficult to maintain when we see our planet as a fragile blue crescent fading to become an inconspicuous point of light against the unimaginable breadth of the universe of celestial gases, black holes, dark matter, stars, planets, galaxies, quasars, and so forth.

With due respect to the great musical artist John Lennon, imagining there are no countries *is* hard to do. However, I have imagined it, and I'm not the only one. On September 21, 1987, President Ronald Reagan, in a speech to the UN, said:

> Can we and all nations not live in peace? In our obsession with antagonisms of the moment, we often forget how much unites all the members of humanity. Perhaps we need some outside, universal threat to make us recognize this common bond. I occasionally think how quickly our differences worldwide would vanish if we were facing an alien threat from outside this world. And yet, I ask you, is not an alien force already among us? What could be more alien to the universal aspirations of our peoples than war and the threat of war? (Reagan 1987, para. 35)

We have become accustomed to fighting wars over portions of land and the resources that land offers. However, slowly but surely the countries of the Earth, separated by imaginary boundaries, have become more and more dependent upon each other. Humankind is irretrievably headed toward the reality of living on an Earth whose ecosystem is interrelated and interdependent. That is the reality where it is not the artificial countries that we have defined for ourselves that matter, but simply our survival on this relatively isolated planet. Yes, this means living in harmony and synergy with the blessings that Earth has to offer to help us survive. We are quickly converging toward the time when we will be forced to cooperate and interconnect as peoples, not as countries. We can all think of the reasons for this convergence because they are becoming obvious.

Our planet is becoming warmer and some of the reasons for that global warming are due to us. That rise in temperature is causing changes in our weather, our water, and food supplies. It is also changing the ocean levels, which will impact our living space. To reverse this, we must cooperate.

Our obsession with protecting our national boundaries has resulted in many wars among ourselves. The associated lust for more lethal weapons to kill each other has brought us to the point where we now have the means to completely destroy every living thing on our planet. To reverse this, we must cooperate.

Governments of our planet are hiding more and more secrets from their people. This breeds corruption and isolation from the people. It creates a scenario where special interests of those in power are paramount instead of the peoples' interests. To reverse this, we must cooperate.

On December 18, 2010, hundreds of youthful protestors rioted near Tunis, Tunisia, in discontent over high unemployment and after a fruit vendor set himself on fire in protest over the confiscation of his fruit stand by the local police. This incident sparked more protests and riots in the country in the weeks that followed. It also sparked riots in Egypt and Algeria. On January 14, 2011, the government of Tunisia was overthrown. Thus began what was known as the "Arab Spring." By February 11, 2011, Mubarak of Egypt had been ousted after weeks of intense rioting by the populace. However, well after Mubarak's departure, the people continued to protest the military rule. By September 2011, Gaddafi of Libya had been deposed after intense fighting by rebel forces. And the civil war in Syria, though subsiding, has been going since March 2011.

What can we, the people, yearning to live free, learn from these historic events? What is clear from a historical perspective is that there are limits to what people will tolerate as what they see are abuses of power from their government. The governments involved in the Arab Spring were not seen as democracies. They were seen as autocratic by their peoples. However, even in countries that are seen as having democratic forms of government, there are certainly abuses of power. Democratic governments are still a work in progress. In addition, each democratic country has its unique methods of government.

Let us look briefly at the US system. Currently there are certain aspects of our government that are ripe for corruption. The Defense Department is the prime suspect because they receive the lion's share of funding.

There has been an enormous burden of keeping too many secrets. What is the scale of our secrets? In US government agencies, there are currently more than two thousand individuals who have the authority to make an original classification of TOP SECRET or below. We have become a nation of secrets!

What harm does too much secrecy do?

Holding secrets is power. Power corrupts. If corruption in government spreads, very soon you have a government replete with corruption. If that happens, the people will suffer because their interests will not be considered. Only the interests of the powerful will matter. We have to consider the potential long-term effects from allowing excessive secrecy to flourish. New technology, for example, is lost to the public when it is kept secret from them due to its potential military application. That hurts the public at large and keeps the focus on military superiority.

What about the character of a country? If we present ourselves as the leaders of the free world, shouldn't we be seen as having some qualities that will bring the world of nations together? The only way we will truly become a world working cooperatively is if the countries of the world demonstrate the qualities we all admire: fairness, honesty, equal treatment, mutual respect, openness, and accountability to the people. Moreover, these admirable traits in the governments of countries can only be achieved through the demands of its people. That means you and me taking an active role in oversight of our governments. In the United States, we have the opportunity to exercise our freedoms, if only we will. If we do not, we allow the status quo to continue. If we do nothing, we allow excessive secrecy, we allow corruption to take hold, we allow unnecessary wars to happen, we allow a few to control us and our lives without our consent, and we allow a few to decide how we will interact with extraterrestrial life.

CHAPTER 10

The Recurring Risk of Nuclear War

"What nowadays is euphemistically called national defense, in fact always includes preparations for attack, and thus constitutes a threat to some other group of people. This type of defense assumes that threats directed towards other people will produce in them either submission, or negotiation, or avoidance. It neglects the possibility that contempt or retaliation may be produced instead. Yet, in fact the usual effect between comparable nations is retaliation by counter-preparations, thus leading on by way of an arms race towards another war."
—LEWIS RICHARDSON, "MATHEMATICS OF WAR AND FOREIGN POLITICS" (1956, 1243)

THE ESCALATING RISK

Until recently, the public had become somewhat indifferent to the fact that there are thousands of nuclear weapons available to nine different countries that could begin a nuclear war at any moment. With the recent spate of threats from Russia of using tactical nukes in their war in

Ukraine, the public is now taking seriously the possibility of nuclear war. Of course, a nuclear war would be a completely catastrophic extinction event for many species, including our own.

Because of the ongoing war in Ukraine, NATO has taken a more significant role. In addition to Ukraine's formal request to join NATO, at least two other nations (Finland and Sweden) have formally requested to join NATO because of threat posed by Russian aggression. NATO nations have supplied military intelligence, advice, and weaponry to Ukraine, and today Ukrainian forces appear determined to recover all land that has been taken by Russian aggression. However, the war has not ended, and questions remain as to the extent Russia will go to achieve a semblance of victory.

Russia has used civilian nuclear power plants as weapons of war. During the Ukraine war, they threatened the release of radiation from captured plants, which would also have threatened the lives of people in European nations. It may be an idle threat at this point, but what of the future?

NATO nations have long held tactical nuclear weapons (TNW) as a deterrent against Russia using their own. In the early stages of the Ukraine war, the Western powers made statements to the effect that if Russia were to use TNW, it would be a line crossed, and NATO forces might have to engage. To date, Russia has not used TNW, but that does not preclude their use sometime in the future if they perceive a direct threat from NATO. The question of the potential use of TNW will not be answered from the result of this war.

Whatever the outcome, Russia and the West will still have nuclear arsenals that include TNW and strategic nuclear weapons! The war in Ukraine may, for now, resolve border issues, but it will not have resolved the question of the potential use of nukes in future disputes between nations. In fact, other nations may now see the validity of obtaining TNW as a deterrence. The danger is that, as long as nuclear deterrence is some sort of desirable security blanket, nations will want to possess the weapons, and the potential use of them in conflicts will increase simply because of the number of weapons available.

On February 4, 2021, the New Start treaty providing the limitation of nuclear weapons by the Russian Federation and the United States was renewed. It now provides for the following aggregate limits:

- 700 deployed intercontinental ballistic missiles (ICBMs), deployed submarine-launched ballistic missiles (SLBMs), and deployed heavy bombers equipped with nuclear armaments,

- 800 deployed and non-deployed ICBM launchers, SLBM launchers, and heavy bombers equipped for nuclear armaments, and

- 1,550 nuclear warheads on deployed ICBMs, deployed SLBMs, and deployed heavy bombers equipped with nuclear armaments.

The treaty also provides for verification and transparency measures, including onsite inspections, data exchange, and production notifications. The treaty has been extended until 2026.

Notwithstanding the stated restrictions and verification measures, both the US and Russia have a much greater stockpile of nuclear weapons that are not deployed. And, as with any treaty, the New Start treaty can be broken at any time based on the will of either party. Moreover, there are no provisions to begin a further reduction in nuclear arms. In fact, the opposite is true. Both nations are intent on improving and modernizing their nuclear forces. One concern is that both nations are developing more tactical nuclear weapons with the potential for use in "limited" warfare.

In a statement from the 2020 US Strategic Command (USSTRATCOM) report by commander Gen. Charles Richard:

> To be clear, nuclear deterrence is the highest priority mission of the Department of Defense—our deterrent underwrites every U.S. military operation around the world and is the foundation and backstop of our national defense.
>
> The ability of the United States to deter threats to our Nation and our Allies is at a critical point. The contemporary security environment is the most challenging since the Cold War. In the nuclear dimension, we face a range of potential adversaries, each with different interests, objectives, and capabilities. To maintain a credible deterrent in this environment requires us to modernize and recapitalize our strategic forces to ensure our Nation has the capability to deter any actor, at any level. (Richard 2020, intro.)

In June 2020, Russian president Putin approved an equally definitive statement in their document "Basic Principles of State Policy of the Russian Federation on Nuclear Deterrence": "The Russian Federation considers nuclear weapons exclusively as a means of deterrence."

However, this document allows for use of nuclear weapons if there is aggression against the Russian Federation even if conventional weapons are used. In addition, Russian officials have made statements that their real doctrine goes beyond basic deterrence and toward regional war-fighting strategies.

Both the US and Russia have committed to further modernization and development of "low-yield" tactical nuclear weapons for use in regional conflicts. This begs the question: If these tactical nuclear weapons were used in any conflict, would that be considered a First Strike of nuclear weaponry and thereby give an opponent the justification to retaliate in kind? How long would it be before the conflict would escalate to the use of larger-yield nukes?

General John "Jay" Raymond (n.d.), the first commander of the U.S. Space Command, said, "We have acknowledged that Space is a warfighting domain, similar to air, land, and sea. Now we must organize and develop the joint force to posture for space superiority across the continuum of conflict—and the work is ongoing." Will we next take nuclear weapons into the space domain and to future bases on other worlds?

Further complicating this issue is the unpredictable threat that other nuclear nations may use the weapons in their regional conflicts.

According to a recent report from Mr. Sabir Hussain, director of the Indian Society for UFO Studies (INSUFOS): "India and Pakistan have fought four wars over Kashmir (1947, 1965, 1971, 1999) since partition in 1947." Since the late 1980s, there have been insurgencies going on in Kashmir, where ISIS-trained militants have been carrying out regular attacks on Indian military bases as part of their policy.

India and Pakistan have conducted open nuclear weapons tests. Since 2003, India has started deploying nuclear missiles while Pakistan has deployed six land-based nuclear missiles and battlefield tactical nukes.

As of today, both India and Pakistan are involved in an open nuclear arms race with each having acquired nuclear first-strike capabilities and on the verge of acquiring second- and third-strike capabilities from land-, air-, and sea-based platforms. Even though in 2003 India announced a "No Nuclear First Use" policy, since 2013, after Modi became prime minister, statements coming from the highest levels of Indian government indicate that a first-strike scenario is not off the table.

In 2018, General Zubair Mahmood Hayat, chairman of the Joint Chiefs of Staff of the Pakistani army, warned that if Israel tries to attack Pakistan, then they will wipe out the Zionist regime in less than twelve minutes. The Shaheen 3 missile has a range more than twenty-seven hundred kilometers and can reach Israel. In addition, groups like ISIS or Al-Qaeda will not hesitate to take control of Pakistani nuclear missiles if they can. To date, they have made six unsuccessful attempts. In some cases, they had inside help in their attempts, including from the base commander himself.

In September 2022, Russian president Vladimir Putin publicly threatened to use "tactical" nuclear weapons (5–10 kt) in the war with Ukraine. The US countered those threats simply by stating that there would be very serious (undefined) consequences if Russia did use such weapons. Clearly, the status of the New Start Treaty is now in doubt. In October 2022, North Korea tested more mid-range and long-range nuclear-capable missiles, further establishing themselves as a nuclear weapons power.

The preamble to the NPT clearly expressed humanity's hopes to live without fear of a nuclear holocaust. However, there were no words on how to truly accomplish such peaceful coexistence. That is because living in peace must be an organic process. It must be something within us that drives us to cooperate among ourselves to solve such profound issues that could result in our self-extinction. We cannot evolve as a civilization and have a peaceful future unless we clearly demonstrate our respect and love for each other. We will need to show that we recognize the value of all life.

From the untold number of confirmed sightings of UAP, it is obvious that ETs want us to know they are here. It is obvious they are concerned with the level of risk we have created for ourselves with nuclear weapons. It may be that they have focused on this risk to the catastrophic mass extinction of our species and many others on earth because they have seen it on other worlds. It is likely they have learned how to avoid such catastrophic wars. Why haven't they simply landed, extended their greetings, and given us advice on living in peace? They have already demonstrated they have the technology to disable any of our nuclear weapons. Why not simply present us with that technology as a peaceful gesture?

ETs have already done us a favor by combining the evidence of their presence with their focus on the weapons we have created for our own extinction. They have also done us the favor of not interfering with the relations we have with one another to resolve our problems and achieve peaceful coexistence. Clearly our species must take decisive actions for itself.

In the present, we have an opportunity to motivate those actions. We are being observed by ET species, and our governments know it. There has been a long history of keeping this profound secret from us. Government agencies may again attempt to minimize what they know. We cannot allow governments to obfuscate, minimize, or hide that information. We, the people, must assert our right to know all that has been discovered about UAP.

CHAPTER 11

Endemic Excessive Secrecy in Government

In the US, the government has the absolute power to withhold information from the public. This power is derived from the preamble to the Constitution where it establishes the need for our government to "provide for the common defense . . . and secure the blessings of liberty." In other words, provide for and secure our national security. Thus, secrecy in government is inviolate. Our government will have its secrets. The Constitution does not speak to how much secrecy is necessary or if excessive secrecy could be detrimental to our democracy.

Every year, the president receives a report from the Information Security Oversight Office (ISOO), the agency whose mission includes "ensuring that the government protects and allows proper access to classified and controlled unclassified information to advance the national and public interest." In the most recent report, Director Mark Bradley stated the following: "I believe more than ever that Americans must have faith in their government's honesty and openness. . . . Fear and ignorance, the most corrosive and dangerous of all acids for a republic, will continue to eat away at the strength and resilience of our governing pillars if we do not neutralize them with candor and transparency" (ISOO 2022, 3).

The "2021 Annual Report to the President" (ISOO 2022, 5–20) identified the following deficiencies in security programs:

- The "tsunami" of digital classified information being created daily makes it likely that most of it will never be reviewed for declassification (5).

- There are inconsistencies in creating and maintaining Special Access Programs (SAPs) and Controlled Access Programs (CAPs). There is little oversight of these programs to ensure agencies are appropriately establishing and administering them (6).

- There is an urgent need to update the primary national security authorities (offices and individuals who have the authority to classify information) that govern the Classified National Security Information (CNSI) system (10).

- ISOO was unable to determine the number of "derivative" classification actions because of the varied approaches agencies use. They have therefore ended this requirement. Derivative classification is information that is classified due to its relationship to "original" classification of information. For the same reasons, ISOO has dropped reporting requirements for the number of Original Classification Authorities (OCA) by agencies (11–12).

- Agencies have little incentive to complete requests for appeals on time, resulting in more appeals (12).

- The DOD is responsible for 73.5 percent of the 2,116 total security classification guides (SCG) used by federal agencies. It has taken ISOO two years to review 130 of these DOD SCGs. Their finding is that 26.1 percent were deficient in the listing the OCA. In 14.6 percent, the rationale for classification was not provided. In 20.7 percent, the fixed date for declassification was not provided as required (13).

- ISOO points to a significant concern where sixteen of the SCGs that include exemptions to the automatic declassification at twenty-five years, the OCA responsible for the SCG does not have the authority to apply an exemption. "SCGs are the primary means for OCAs to make classification decisions and are essential to the proper functioning of the classification system. They are also the fundamental tool used for derivative classification—that is, carrying forward the classification decisions made by OCAs—which accounts for the overwhelming majority of classification actions." Deficient or inaccurate SCGs leads to the proliferation of illegitimate classified information and enables information to be classified at the wrong level (13–14).

- In fiscal year 2021, sixteen agencies have designated 671 Top Secret level OCAs and 817 Secret level OCAs (14).

- The DOD is responsible for inspecting and monitoring contractors, licensees, and grantees under the CNSI. This is identified as the National Industrial Security Program. There are thirty-nine agencies across the executive branch that have classified contracts. This program needs an overhaul as it is almost thirty years old and, according to ISOO, no longer supports our national security needs (18).

- The Public Interest Declassification Board (PIDB) was established to conduct declassification reviews. Because Congress has been using the PIDB as a preferred vehicle for conducting declassification reviews without the expenditure of funds, the administrative cost burden has become significant on ISOO. ISOO cannot sustain their support without additional resources (20).

These have been persistent issues of the CNSI, spanning decades. The deficiencies in the classification system are endemic and the system has been operating with gross inefficiencies. A long-standing, organized group from within, such as a UFO secrecy cabal, would be well aware of these shortcomings and could use them to their advantage to maintain secrecy.

How do these "corrosive effects" impact the disclosure of information on UAP? First, it allows the complexity and pitfalls of the system to delay issuing information. Any release of information would require review by the OCA and its concurrence that releasing it would not disclose sources and methods. And then it would require coordination between agencies to further validate the release. This could involve at least sixteen other agencies!

For example, a portion of the current legislative requirements for the study of UAP under the National Defense Authorization act reads:

(e) . . . (2) INTELLIGENCE COLLECTION AND ANALYSIS PLAN

The head of the Office . . . , acting on behalf of the Secretary of Defense and the Director of National Intelligence, shall supervise the development and execution of an intelligence collection and analysis plan to gain as much knowledge as possible regarding the technical and operational characteristics, origins, and intentions of unidentified aerial phenomena, including with respect to the development, acquisition, deployment, and operation of technical collection capabilities necessary to detect, identify, and scientifically characterize unidentified aerial phenomena. (U.S. Code: Title 50, n.d., § 3373)

This activity alone would require the establishment of more classification of data because it involves "sources and methods." All the deficiencies in the classification system would still be in place and worsen the "tsunami" of digital classified information.

Notwithstanding the deficiencies in the system, the question is whether or not individual officers, such as the president, members of Congress, or heads of agencies, will allow the people to know what information they have in their possession. Will they take the actions needed to reform the system and give the public access to what they ought to know?

In 2011, President Obama issued directives to federal agencies for greater government transparency. As part of that effort, he offered to respond to public inquiries on any topic. I and others took the opportunity to request all information held by government agencies on the question of whether there was evidence of visitation to earth by extraterrestrial civilizations. The official response was released through the Office of Science and Technology and endorsed by the White House. The response was: "The U.S. government has no evidence that any life exists outside our planet, or that an extraterrestrial presence has contacted or engaged any member of the human race" (Atkinson 2011).

In 2021, Obama's position seemed to have changed. In a *Late Late Show* interview, he said, "We don't know exactly what they are, we can't explain how they moved, their trajectory. They did not have an easily explainable pattern. And so, you know, I think that people still take seriously trying to investigate and figure out what that is" (Cillizza 2021).

In truth, the question of an extraterrestrial presence is a simple calculus: from the overwhelming number of observations by credible witnesses such as pilots and other direct observers, these objects perform aerial maneuvers that are impossible for human-manufactured craft to perform or for any human pilot to withstand. These observations have been made for decades. There has been no evidence presented that any nation on earth has built such craft. Therefore, it is entirely logical that they were not manufactured on earth. Why is this simple logic so difficult for governments to acknowledge?

The apparent model for keeping secrets relies on the proposition that governments can operate more efficiently and effectively within a large, durable bubble of secrecy. Part of this model is that there are bubbles within bubbles; that is, compartmentalization, which keeps secrets contained in tight, need-to-know groups.

The essential principle of this model is that secrets are necessary for protection from or to gain an advantage over our real or perceived enemies.

There are also benefits that accrue to the holders. Secrets create power and influence. That power and influence can become strongly corruptive. When that happens, the people lose control of and access to government. That is a detriment to a free and democratic society. The people are forced to live by the decisions made by a select few.

Because of the internet and social media, we are now in a new stage of the information age. People are hungry for real and "true" information. We have seen the results of too much secrecy, resulting in the proliferation of conspiracy theories and "fake news"—all because the people were kept in the dark through an excesses of secrecy.

To effectively fight excessive secrecy in government, we need whistleblowers. We need people to step up, risking their reputations and livelihoods, to inform us about these secrets. This will continue to happen when the burden of certain secrets becomes too overwhelming. When people who hold secrets realize there is a greater interest at stake—that of the people over that of government bureaucrats—more will be revealed.

The secrecy apparatus of governments is large, complex, and cumbersome and cannot be completely controlled—as has recently been demonstrated. Governments cannot continue to "shortchange" or "sanitize" the truth. The public wants a complete story of UAP, as it is, irrespective of how that truth might be perceived.

EPILOGUE

Think of the last war you can remember when you were aware that someone you knew had died or had been wounded. It may be painful to think about it. But now take it further. Try to envision the face of a soldier who is mentally tormented by having experienced war or the face of a child terrorized by war. Try to see the face of each and every one who has suffered from war and the different ways they suffered. Try to imagine the burned skin of those who lived through the horror of the atomic bomb at Hiroshima or Nagasaki. We have all seen enough—too much human suffering.

Now imagine the possibility that you and I have the power to keep this kind of suffering from ever happening again. You may say that's impossible—that we are powerless to stop a nuclear war. But that is exactly what we must do, individually and together. If each of us commits to the idea of the complete and total abolition of nuclear weapons, together we will have prevented nuclear war.

It is not just nuclear weapons that should concern us. All of us have a need to know about all sciences that could impact our lives: socially, economically, even our very existence. This means opening scientific discoveries to all so that humanity can work together to use science for the good of all humankind, not for the creation of more advanced weapons. Yes, this would mean governments would have to tell some of their secrets. It would need governments to open up to one another and share knowledge about one another.

If there were fewer secrets among countries, no weapons of mass destruction to worry about, and nations working cooperatively to solve world problems instead of threatening one another, then governments would have no excuse to hold secret the UFO phenomenon. The world would be unified in deciding how to meet the challenge of working in harmony with beings from other worlds. Then we will have evolved and can move forward as a peaceful civilization of the cosmos.

You may say that I'm a dreamer, but I hope I am not the only one.

ADDENDUM—OCTOBER 2022

We witnesses deserve to be heard. Certainly by the people of our country but also by the people of the world. Those of us who have come forward deserve the respect of acknowledgment of this reality.

I think what it boils down to is this question: Who Are We?

If we were to encounter an "advanced" civilization on another planet, our first question might be: Who are they? What do they think about war, self-protection, social interactions, the purpose of life, the afterlife, etc. And how might they react to us? Would they consider us a possible enemy? But, ultimately, it would be about what values we have with respect to ourselves and other living creatures.

So, I ask: Who Are We? What are our values?

Currently, we are embroiled in an international crisis with respect to our ability to keep nuclear weapons from being used in warfare. Clearly, we cannot control all the nukes that lie in the hands of various nations. If, for example, Putin uses even a small nuke in his war with Ukraine, humankind will have demonstrated that we are not capable of avoiding a nuclear war of annihilation of all life on this planet. We will have shown ourselves to be void of the necessary character to keep others in our solar system, and beyond, safe from us.

From the ET perspective, I would think they would ask: Why is this civilization fractured into nation-states? Why do they (still) engage in war against one another? Are they evolving toward having a unified culture? If so, what form will that take?

Then I would ask: Are there universal values that we ought to consider? Have we met those requirements? Do we deserve to be part of the family of civilizations in the universe, as defined by some universal standards of being "civil"?

During the May 17, 2022, hearing by the House Subcommittee on Intelligence on the subject of UAP, Ronald Moultrie (Under Secretary of Defense for Intelligence and Security) and Scott Bray (Deputy Director of Naval Intelligence) testified. Mr. Moultrie has been a senior member of the CIA and a senior executive with the NSA and the NRO, the most secret organizations in the USGOV. Notably, he has no scientific credentials. Mr. Bray has worked as an intelligence officer since 2004. However, he has worked under the Director for Naval Intelligence for only two years. He also has no scientific degree or experience. Since the unidentified aerial phenomenon is one that defies our current understanding of many fields of science, it seems incongruent that these two would be selected to testify about attempting to explain it. Indeed, no definitive answers came from their testimonies.

Although I have spoken openly of the Malmstrom events for over twenty-six years and have recently sent letters to members of Congress offering to give them in-person briefings about the incidents, none have accepted my offer. It may be the case that they don't want to receive information that the intelligence community might consider classified.

Because the UFO cabal has been operating for decades within the organs of government, many more individuals and agencies of government are well aware of their existence. The greater the size and scope of the organization, the greater the risk of revealing knowledge of its existence and its modus operandi. This may offer the opportunity to seek out whistleblowers or a "Deep Throat."

Bent AARO

On February 15, 2023, I gave a nearly two-hour interview to the US government office designated to research and report on the UAP issue. This is the All-Domain Anomaly Resolution Office (AARO). The establishment of AARO within the US Department of Defense (DOD) is the result of what was initially the Unidentified Aerial Phenomena Task Force (UAPTF) that was tasked under the 2021 National Defense Authorization Act (NDAA).

The Office of the Director of National Intelligence (ODNI) issued the "Preliminary Assessment: Unidentified

Aerial Phenomena" on June 25, 2021. It concluded, in part, "UAP clearly pose a safety of flight issue and may pose a challenge to U.S. national security" (3). It also stated they "currently lack data to indicate any UAP are . . . indicative of a major technological advancement by a potential adversary" (6). AARO has now an official record of the testimony of Robert Jacobs, which involves video of an unidentified controlled object flying at very high speeds while circling a simulated nuclear warhead in flight. AARO also has my official testimony describing UFOs disabling nuclear missiles on two separate occasions. These two official records alone should constitute data sufficient to indicate that UAP constitute major technological advancements that could be a challenge to national security.

Section 1683 of the 2022 NDAA established a requirement for an office, within DOD, to carry out the duties of the UAPTF. One of those specified tasks required reporting on "The number of reported incidents, and descriptions thereof, of unidentified aerial phenomena associated with military nuclear assets, including strategic nuclear weapons" (117th Congress 2021, 135, STAT. 2121–2122, [h][2][M])

My testimony, now an official record, to AARO spoke specifically of two incidents involving the disabling of strategic nuclear weapons. I also informed them of the importance of an additional very similar incident that occurred at Minot AFB, ND, in September 1966. They were aware of that incident and indicated their intent to contact the principal witness for his statement. The facts of these three incidents, occurring within the span of six months and resulting in the disabling of thirty nuclear weapons during UFO encounters, can no longer be denied, or ignored, by AARO or any other government agency giving serious deliberations to UAP around nuclear weapons facilities.

Some aspects of my interview with AARO are concerning. When I specifically asked them if they would be checking details of my presentation with the Air Force (AF), the reply was "not directly." They indicated that they were having trouble obtaining information. Many of their inquiries had a standard evasive response of: "Everything the AF has to say is a matter of record." AARO indicated they would leave it up to the Congress to sort out the validity of any official record such as my presentation.

In my opinion, this approach is totally insufficient. In each of the incidents I presented, there were multiple witnesses and substantial documentation to verify the facts. Many of the principal witnesses are still living. Resolution of these facts and acknowledgment through a summary statement by the principal government agency should be required in order to complete the historical and public record.

I am concerned that our government has adopted the philosophy that the less the public knows, the easier it is to govern. This seems to be a serious flaw in the furtherance of the ideals of democracy. We should all protest such a philosophy. In particular, we should protest being kept in the dark about the facts surrounding the very real possibility that we are indeed being visited by highly intelligent sentient beings from elsewhere. Our future relationship with such beings could be critical to our survival. We have a need to know.

REFERENCES

117th Congress. 2021. "S.1605 – National Defense Authorization Act for Fiscal Year 2022." *congress.gov.*

Aftergood, Steven. 1989. "Background on Space Nuclear Power." *Science & Global Security* 1, nos. 1–2.

AHF (Atomic Heritage Foundation). 2022. "Groves & Farrell Watching Trinity." *ahf.nuclearmuseum.org.*

Atkinson, Nancy. 2011. "White House: There's No Sign of E.T. or UFO Cover-up." *Universe Today,* available at NBC News website, *nbcnews.com.*

Bird, Kai, and Martin J. Sherwin. 2005. *American Prometheus.* New York: Alfred A. Knopf.

Birnes, William J., ed. 2004. *The UFO Magazine UFO Encyclopedia.* New York: Pocket Books.

Brumfiel, Geoff. 2011. "Military Surveillance Data: Shared Intelligence." *Nature* 477 (7365): 388–389, *nature.com.*

Burr, William, and David Alan Rosenberg. 2010. "Nuclear Competition in an Era of Stalemate, 1963–1975." In *The Cambridge History of the Cold War Volume II,* edited by Melvyn P. Leffler and Odd Arne Westad. Cambridge: Cambridge University Press.

Carey, Thomas J., and Donald R. Schmitt. 2009. *Witness to Roswell.* Franklin Lakes, NJ: New Page Books.

Chase, Lieutenant Colonel Lewis. 1967a. Memo to Colonel James Manatt, Foreign Technology Division, Wright-Patterson Air Force Base. *the ufochronicles.com.*

———. 1967b. Trip report regarding the meeting at the University of Colorado between the Condon Committee and the (Air Force) Base UFO Investigators.

Cillizza, Chris. 2021. "Barack Obama Just Said Something *Very* Interesting about UFOs." CNNWire, *cnn.com.*

Craig, Roy. 1995. *UFOs: An Insider's View of the Official Quest for Evidence.* Denton, TX: University of North Texas Press.

CRS (Congressional Research Service). 2010. "The New START Treaty: Central Limits and Key Provisions." Report R41219 (September 20). Every CRS Report, *everycrsreport.com.*

————. 2011. "The State Secrets Privilege: Preventing the Disclosure of Sensitive National Security Information During Civil Litigation." Report R41741 (March 28). Every CRS Report, *everycrsreport.com*.

Cutler, Robert. 1958. "19. Letter from the President's Special Assistant for National Security Affairs (Cutler) to Secretary of State Dulles." In the "Summary of Conclusions." Office of the Historian, historical documents, *history.state.gov*.

Druffel, Ann. 2003. *Firestorm: Dr. James E. McDonald's Fight for UFO Science*. Columbus, NC: Wild Flower Press.

Durant, F. C. 1953. "The Durant Report of the Robertson Panel Proceedings." *cufon.org*.

Dworshak, Leo. 2003. *UFOs Are with Us: Take My Word*. Pittsburgh, PA: Dorrance Publishing Co.

FAS (Federation of American Scientists) et al. 2013. Letter to President Barack Obama. "Re: Security Classification Reform Steering Committee." April 23. *sgp.fas.org*.

Faulconbridge, Guy. 2012. "Report: Russian Nuclear Disaster Narrowly Averted in Submarine Fire." *Huffington Post*, February 14. *www.huffpost.com*.

Feschino, Frank C., Jr. 2007. *Shoot Them Down*. Lulu Enterprises, *www.lulu.com*.

Friedman, Stanton, and Kathleen Marden. 2007. *Captured*. Franklin Lakes, NJ: New Page Books.

Gamble, David. 1967. "USAF 341st Strategic Missile Wing." In "UFO Case: Malmstrom AFB/UFO Missile Incident (March 16, 1967)" by John Greenewald (March 4, 2015). The Black Vault, *documents.theblackvault.com*.

Good, Timothy. 1988. *Above Top Secret: The Worldwide UFO Cover-Up*. New York: Quill, William Morrow.

Gottron, Frank, and Dana A. Shea. 2013. "Publishing Scientific Papers with Potential Security Risks: Issues for Congress." Congressional Research Service, *crsreports.congress.gov*.

Griffioen, Alex. 2018. "The Soesterberg UFO, 1979." UFO Zaken (Netherlands), *ufozaken.nl*.

Hall, Richard. 1988. *Uninvited Guests: A Documented History of UFO Sightings, Alien Encounters, and Coverups*. Santa Fe, N.M.: Aurora Press.

Hastings, Robert. 2008. *UFOs and Nukes*. Bloomington, IN: Author House.

Hersey, John. 1946. *Hiroshima.* New York: Vintage Books, Random House.

Hopkins, Budd. 1981. *Missing Time.* New York: Richard Marek Publishers.

ISOO (Information Security Oversight Office). 2022. "2021 Annual Report to the President." *archives.gov/isoo.*

Kerr, Richard A. 2013. "Soot Is Warming the World Even More Than Thought." *Science* 339, no. 6118 (January 25): 382. doi:10.1126/science.339.6118.382.

Leir, Roger. 2005. *The Aliens and the Scalpel.* San Diego, CA: Book Tree.

Low, Robert. 1966. "Some Thoughts on the UFO Project." In "Flying Saucer Fiasco" by John G. Fuller, *Look* magazine, May 14, 1968. *project1947.com.*

Maccabee, Bruce. (1996). "Acceleration." In *MUFON 1996 International UFO Symposium Proceedings: Ufology: A Scientific Enigma,* edited by W. H. Andrus. Seguin, TX: Mutual UFO Network.

Mack, John. 1995. "The UFO Abduction Phenomenon: What Does It Mean for the Transformation of Human Consciousness?" *Primal Renaissance: The Journal of Primal Psychology* 1, no. 1 (Spring): 96–110. Available online at *johnemackinstitute.org.*

McCullough, David. 1992. *Truman.* New York: Simon and Schuster.

Monatt, Colonel James. 1967. Memo to Base Operations Office, Wright-Patterson Air Force Base. *the ufochronicles.com.*

"Multi-Service Doctrine for Chemical, Biological, Radiological, and Nuclear Operations." 2011. FM 3-11/MCWP 3-37.1/NWP 3-11/AFTTP 3-2.42, Defense Department manual. *globalsecurity.org.*

Nalty, Bernard C. n.d. "An Uncommon War: The US Air Force in Southeast Asia." Air Force Historical Support Division. *afhistory.af.mil.*

"New START Treaty." 2011. U.S. Department of State website, *state.gov.*

"NSC-68: United States Objectives and Programs for National Security." 1950. Wilson Center Digital Archive, *digitalarchive .wilsoncenter.org.*

ODNI (Office of the Director of National Intelligence). 2021. "Preliminary Assessment: Unidentified Aerial Phenomena." Intelligence Community Assessments and Reports. *dni.gov.*

Omang, Joanne. 1979. "4,000 Slightly Contaminated Gallons May Have Left Three Mile Island." *Washington Post* online, *washingtonpost.com.*

OWN (Oprah Winfrey Network). 1994. "The Man Who Says He Was Abducted by Aliens." *The Oprah Winfrey Show*. Available on YouTube, *youtube.com*.

Petit, Jean-Pierre, Julien Geffray, and Fabrice David. 2009. "MHD Hypersonic Flow Control for Aerospace Applications." *jp-petit.org*.

Pincus, Walter. 2008. "Eisenhower Advisors Discussed Using Nuclear Weapons in China." *Washington Post* (April 30). Access at Columbian College of Arts & Sciences History News Network, *historynetwork.org*.

Pye, Lloyd. 2010. "2010 Nuclear DNA (nuDNA) Result Discussed." Starchild Project website, *starchildproject.com*.

Raymond, John "Jay." n.d. Home page quote on Air Force Space Command (Archived) website, *afspc.af.mil*.

Reagan, Ronald. 1987. "Address to the 42d Session of the United Nations General Assembly in New York, New York." September 21. *reaganlibrary.gov*.

Reynolds, Tom. 2002. "Final Report of the Hanford Thyroid Disease Study Released." *Journal of the National Cancer Institute* 94, no. 14: 1046–1048. *jnci.oxfordjournals.org*. doi:10.1093/jnci/94.14.1046.

Rhodes, Richard. 1986. *The Making of the Atomic Bomb*. New York: Touchstone.

Richard, Charles A. 2020. "2020 USSTRATCOM Posture Statement." U.S. Strategic Command, *www.stratcom.mil*.

Richardson, Lewis. 1956. "Mathematics of War and Foreign Politics." In *The World of Mathematics*, by James A. Newman. New York: Simon and Schuster.

Richelson, Jeffrey T. 1998. "Scientists in Black." *Scientific American* 278, no. 2 (February): 48–55.

———. 2006. *Spying on the Bomb*. New York: W.W. Norton & Co.

———. 2016. *The U.S. Intelligence Community*. Boulder, Colo.: Westview Press.

Robertson Panel. 1953. (January 14–17). Available online at *www.bibliotecapleyades.net*.

Ruppelt, Edward J. 1956. *The Report on Unidentified Flying Objects*. London: Victor Gollancz.

Sagan, Carl. (1980) 2013. *Cosmos*. New York: Wings Books. Reprint, New York: Ballantine Books. Citations refer to the Ballantine edition.

Salas, Robert, and James Klotz. 2005. *Faded Giant*. Scotts Valley, CA: CreateSpace.

Smith, Yvonne. 2008. *Chosen: Recollections of UFO Abductions through Hypnotherapy*. Nashville: Backstage Entertainment.

Spencer, Michelle, Aadina Ludin, Heather Nelson. 2012. "The Unauthorized Movement of Nuclear Weapons and Mistaken Shipment of Classified Missile Components: An Assessment." Access Number: ADA557097. Defense Technical Information Center, *apps.dtic.mil*.

Stone, Clifford. 2011. *Eyes Only*. Scotts Valley, CA: CreateSpace.

Trento, Joseph J. 2001. *The Secret History of the CIA*. New York: MJF Books.

United Nations. 2008. "Sources and Effects of Ionizing Radiation: Volume II." UNSCEAR website, *www.unscear.org*.

———. 1968. "Treaty on the Non-Proliferation of Nuclear Weapons (NPT)." Office for Disarmament Affairs. *disarmamentunoda.org*.

U.S. Code: Title 50. n.d. "War and National Defense." Chapter 45, subchapter IV, section 3373. Cornell Law School Legal Information Institute, *law.cornell.edu*.

US Department of Defense. 2005. "Doctrine for Joint Nuclear Operations." Joint Publication 3-12. Final Coordination (2), March 15, 2005. *globalsecurity.org*.

USAF Fact Sheet. 2005. "Unidentified Flying Objects and the Air Force Project Blue Book." *af.mil/About-Us/Fact-Sheets*.

USDOE (US Department of Energy). 2000. DOE/NV—209 REV 15. "United States Nuclear Tests: July 1945 through September 1992." *osti.gov*.

von Neumann, John, and Oskar Morgenstern. 1944. *Theory of Games and Economic Behavior*. Princeton, NJ: Princeton University Press.

Warren, Larry, and Peter Robbins. 1997. *Left at East Gate*. New York: Cosimo.

Wells, H. G. (1914) 2015. *The World Set Free*. London: Macmillan & Co. Reprint, Scotts Valley, CA: (CreateSpace) Jungle Land Publishing. Citations refer to the Jungle Land edition.

The White House. 2009. "Freedom of Information Act: Memorandum for the Heads of Executive Departments and Agencies." *obamawhitehouse.archives.gov*.

INDEX

ABOUT THE AUTHOR

ROBERT SALAS served on active duty with the US Air Force for seven years after graduation from the US Air Force Academy in 1964. He served at Tyndall AFB (Florida) before his assignment at Malmstrom AFB (Montana) in 1966. He earned a master's degree in aerospace engineering from the Air Force Institute of Technology, Wright-Patterson AFB (Ohio). He also worked with the Titan III Missile Systems program office at Los Angeles AFS. After being honorably discharged from the Air Force in 1971, Mr. Salas briefly worked as an engineer for Martin-Marietta Aerospace and Rockwell International. From 1974 until his retirement in 1995, Mr. Salas worked for the Federal Aviation Administration as an aircraft structures engineer. He is currently employed as a high school mathematics teacher.

Mr. Salas has spoken publicly about the 1967 UFO/ Missile Shutdowns since 1995.